Books by Matthew Lowes

Spirituality

That Which is Before You (2020)
When You are Silent It Speaks (Coming in 2021)

Fiction

The End of All Things (2018)

Games

Elements of Chess (2012)
Dungeon Solitaire: Labyrinth of Souls (2016)
Dungeon Solitaire: Devil's Playground (2018)

THAT WHICH IS BEFORE YOU

THAT WHICH IS BEFORE YOU

MATTHEW LOWES

AN INVITATION TO ENLIGHTENMENT

Empty Press

2020

That Which is Before You:
An Invitation to Enlightenment
/ Matthew Lowes
ISBN 978-1-952073-00-7 (pbk.)

Typeset in
Minion Pro by Robert Slimbach
Source Sans pro by Paul D. Hunt

Empty Press

matthewlowes.com

TABLE OF CONTENTS

The biggest secret in the world
is the one you keep from yourself.

PREFACE

I here bear witness to what the great mystics have already reported.

There is nothing but the limitless One, in which all phenomena manifest, and all phenomena are nothing but the One, without division or distinction.

The ultimate reality revealed through enlightenment has gone by many names within various spiritual traditions, but the truth they speak of is beyond all words, all thoughts, all concepts.

This book contains an account of awakening, transformative insights, nascent teachings, and guidance for spiritual practice. May it be of some use in bringing illumination, true happiness, and an end to suffering.

ACKNOWLEDGEMENTS

Thanks to J. Krishnamurti, Alan Watts, and Wolfgang Kopp, among others, whose words, along with those of many ancient texts, pointed beyond the veil of illusions. Thanks to Richard Hittleman, whose words long ago provided an introduction to meditation. Thanks to Alejandro Jodorowsky, whose words inspired an act of magic.

Thanks to Joel Morwood for assuring me that I wasn't crazy, for his wisdom and advice, and for his teachings and embodiment of *The Way of Selflessness*. Thanks to Mark Hurwit, Alex Bronstein, and Ryan Quitzow-James for their many hours of conversation, without which I may not have articulated much of what is contained within this book.

Thanks to Kaizen Taki for his generous teachings, to Elizabeth Engstrom for her constant support, and to all my teachers in martial arts, in writing, in school, and in life who have helped me along the way.

Thanks to everyone who read various drafts of this book and assisted with its preparation.

Thanks to my family, friends, and loved ones.

I am grateful beyond all measure.

THAT WHICH IS BEFORE YOU

Introduction

This is a book about spiritual enlightenment. I never expected to be writing it. Such accounts and teachings have always been around, though. In every age, some people have realized the truth and spoken about it. But enlightenment is still a great secret known only to a few. Even those who know about it or believe it is possible, cannot *really* know until the secret is revealed, for it is a secret you keep from yourself.

The ideas in this book are not intended to challenge any particular spiritual path, nor any process or theory of science. But there is a reality that transcends everything, and that is the subject here. Various religions likely have their roots in a realization of this reality, but the realization has been subsequently interpreted, reinterpreted, misinterpreted, and mythologized. Certainly science is making observations, predictions, and conceptual models of phenomena that arise within this reality. However, to actually see this reality we must doubt everything and seek knowledge directly. Things may not be what they seem, but in the realm of what is, there are no obstructions.

I am not a religious expert, a philosopher, or a scientist. Although I've read a little in each of these fields, I claim no authority except direct realization, insight, and experience. And while I will attempt to make all this clear, I assert no beliefs, nor is there anything in particular I wish you to believe or do. If at times I speak dramatically or persuasively, it is not to support any belief whatsoever. It is rather an attempt to help you see for yourself what I'm talking about. Anything else falls short of the mark.

So whoever you are, see the truth, all at once, in this moment, and a great secret will be revealed to you. Just see what's really happening. See through it all and your troubles are over. If after that you are still a seeker, read on and redouble your efforts! Exhaust every possibility until you finally see it. And if you are a skeptic like I was, I invite you to consider my story. You may think I have something to gain by telling it, but I assure you I do not. I want nothing more than to watch the wind in the trees, and to follow the changes of an ever-changing sky.

PART I

AWAKENING

There it is ...
Grasp its tail and it will sprout ten thousand tails.
Grab its arm and it will grow ten thousand arms.
Fix its gaze and it will open ten thousand eyes.
Charge at it and it will recede from you.
Run away and it will follow.
You cannot escape it.
You cannot master it.
What more can you do?

Something Extraordinary
Happened

What if I told you there was a completely different way of living, in which all the usual anxieties, fears, and confusions of life would no longer trouble you? Instead, in this life you would experience a profound beauty in the everyday world, and you would be filled with a mysterious joy, an unspeakable bliss. What if I told you that in some sense you are the very fabric of reality itself, at one with everything that is, has been, or ever will be, and that it's possible to realize this in such a way that you will wake up, as if from the dull dream of your former life, into the remarkable truth of your own divine nature?

Personally, I wouldn't have believed it. I would have thought that sounds delusional, and anybody making such a claim must be willfully deluding others, unconsciously deluding themselves, or engaging in some combination thereof. I would have thought all that, until the spring of 2016, when at the age of forty-three, as new light sprang from the long darkness of winter, something extraordinary happened to me, totally and permanently transforming my life — something so amazing, so unimaginable, so wonderful, that no amount of hyperbole, or indeed any words at all, could even begin to describe it. But because it may help you to see it for yourself, or at least recognize the possibility of seeing it, I'm going to try to tell you everything I can.

When this happened, I was amazed beyond belief, first that it was actually happening, and then that there was no end to it. But I had no words to describe it. I was aware other people weren't seeing what I was seeing, but I had no way to convey what it was to them. It was beyond all thought, beyond all words, without definable qualities, inexpressible by any philosophy, doctrine, or conceptual model, and unknowable except through direct perception. And yet, we have to call it something if we're going to discuss it.

People call it enlightenment, gnosis, liberation, Self-realization, God-realization, or simply awakening. I won't dispute the vocabulary. It's the one we have. There are many other names for it and many words associated with it, coming from a wide variety of cultures and traditions, but the truth they speak of is beyond all names and words. As a writer, I cannot shy away from using words, but I use them now as a poet does, to evoke something that is truly beyond words themselves. Try to remember this if you find yourself hung up on semantics or any linguistic, philosophical, doctrinal, conceptual, or scientific technicality. However precise I may try to be, I speak as a poet speaks.

That being said, I will be as honest, as plain, as precise, and as frank as I can be about what happened to me, the insights and experiences of this realization, and the possibility for others to undergo the same transformation. But it should be understood throughout, for reasons that will hopefully become clear, that this is not a self-help book, and that the truth I speak of cannot possibly be described. The best I can do is try to point toward the inexpressible, with the hope that you will see it for yourself.

It could take a moment; it could take a lifetime. Ultimately, though, it is inevitable.

An Account of my Awakening

I didn't really believe in any of this stuff. I was very skeptical of anything spiritual. My religious views were agnostic at most, and I didn't think enlightenment was anything more than the fantasies of monks, the power-schemes of religious leaders, and the delusions of druggies, con-artists, and cult leaders. It was not without consideration that I had reached this view. I had been a spiritual seeker, had practiced mediation and religion, and had many experiences that led me to wonder about the nature of reality and the meaning of life. I was always interested in the big questions. But no matter how astonishing the experience or how deep the question, I could never reach any definite conclusion.

Experiences are fleeting, and no matter how seemingly profound, they end. Things return to what seems like normal and we go on with our lives. All our troubles remain, and we still have to get up the next morning and go to school or go to work or whatever. And the big questions ... well, they're really big, and people can spend lifetimes trying to figure them out and never get anywhere. I wasn't any different in this regard. After thousands of years of philosophy, people are still arguing about the same things. There's really no end to it.

Like a lot of people though, I felt like there was something absent in my life, a kind of hole that desperately needed to be filled, a missing thing that I could not place, no matter where I looked. Over time, this developed into deep dissatisfaction, chronic frustration, and eventually depression. And this thing, whatever it was, always seemed just beyond my grasp. It was the only thing that could satisfy me, and it always slipped away, no matter how hard I tried to reach it. And I tried, a thousand different ways I tried — sometimes knowingly, many times unknowingly — to find this missing thing.

At the age of fourteen, I had a spontaneous out-of-body experience. I was walking home alone one night and stopped in the middle of a field to look up at the stars. I lay down in the grass and gazed up in wonder. After a few moments, I seemed to rise out of my body, floating high into the night sky. Disembodied, I could see all around me, and no matter how high I went, I could still see my body clearly on the ground. By thought, I moved, this way and that, higher and higher, but when I considered that I could go right out into space and beyond, fear gripped me. I wondered what would happen to me, and with that thought I returned, as if gradually materializing inside my body. It felt strange to move my arms and legs, but slowly I got up. I remember thinking something incredible had happened, but also that I needed to get home or my parents would wonder where I was.

A few years later, I found a book about meditation and began a series of experiments. I started with a lot of candle gazing, but soon turned my efforts to quieting all thoughts. Nobody told me this was supposed be difficult, so I just set about it, and after a while, I had a profound experience. All thought stopped, and seemingly, I ceased to exist! And yet, consciousness filled a vast darkness, which I recognized as everything ... the unformed totality of the cosmos. I was nowhere, existing and not existing simultaneously, all-knowing and yet knowing nothing. I have no idea how long this experience lasted, but when I came out of it, my normal life and thoughts resumed. I had homework to do, school the next day, and at the time, I suppose I was equally interested in a date with Caitlin Connelly as I was in any sort of cosmic consciousness.

In subsequent years, I had many unusual experiences — out-of-body experiences, lucid dreams, death dreams, beatific visions, hypnagogic sleep paralysis, and what I can say now were flashes of transcendental insight — but I could never make sense of it all. These subjective experiences were just phenomena from which no conclusions could be made. While I was filled with an inexpressible longing, I was also filled with deep skepticism. Surely, all these phenomena could be explained with a scientific, objective model of reality. What I really longed for was the truth, and time and again I was determined not to be fooled wholeheartedly into some unfounded belief.

I continued my experiments with meditation. I read spiritual books. I delved into philosophies and religions. I explored the arts and sciences. I traveled the world in search of myself. I fell into tumultuous romances and endured the deaths of friends and loved ones. I sank into dark depressions and reveled in the chaos of my confusion. I took up and quit a series of careers to pursue my dream of being a writer. I studied and trained in martial arts. I got married and divorced. In short, I got completely lost in life, as we all do. Through it all I was searching for something I couldn't even really articulate. And I struggled endlessly, with the world, with others, and with myself.

Ultimately, this drama of my life — all its circumstances and everything I left out — is really not important, except to say that it was of the utmost importance to my former self. But nothing I ever did, or thought, or tried, relieved the ache in my heart — no relationship, no religion, no philosophy, no idea, no theory, no occupation, no technique. Inwardly, my life began to fall apart. I struggled with depression, and increasingly with a rage unlike anything I had ever known before. When all was said and done, and the trajectory of my life was laid bare before me, it all seemed empty, hollow, worthless.

Eventually I concluded there were no answers to find. There was nothing to do, nowhere to get to, not that would satisfy the insatiable hunger. There was just the hum-drum of life, and coping with all my accumulated baggage. There was no sense to it all, no meaning to my efforts, no end to my pains, and no escape from the life I'd made for myself. I never seriously considered suicide, mostly because I thought of myself as a stubborn person, who would endure to the bitter end, no matter how bitter. But I played with the idea, and I got to a place in life where I understood why some people would go through with it.

While all of this did not seem to be leading anywhere at the time, other than a sense of drudgery, despair, and self-loathing, something else was really going on. My whole life was converging on a point beyond my imagination. All of this was actually leading to awakening.

·❧·

At the age of forty-three, after teaching for a number of years, I was working as an educational assistant at a rural high school in Oregon. It was a low-stress job that allowed me time to write and practice martial arts. My various projects were going well, and I had just achieved some small success with a game I was writing. I was driving fifty minutes to and from work on a winding mountain road to proctor state tests, organize advisor groups, supervise hallways, and run study halls. During the day, as time allowed I would seek refuge in my mind, dreaming up new stories and ideas for games, drawing maps, and pursuing whatever interests arose.

I started meditating again, but not because I thought there was anything to find. I just thought it might help with anxiety and depression. I didn't put much effort into it, maybe fifteen minutes a day when I could fit it in, but it seemed to make some difference. I thought about traveling again, but not with any hope of finding myself — or anything else for that matter. I started reading some spiritual books again, and I was listening to the wonderful lectures of Alan Watts, but with the purely mundane goal of gaining some helpful perspective. It was like I had come full circle. When I was young, I had found spiritual books both fascinating and frustrating. They seemed to speak of this thing that was missing, and yet there was no way to get there. Now that I had given up finding anything, things started making sense in a surprising way.

I began having some unusual thoughts. I realized one day that every imagined limit of myself was completely arbitrary. There were no real boundaries and nothing setting me apart from everything else. And over a number of days I started feeling very strange. I felt unmoored, as if drifting through reality, wandering through each day. At home, startling thoughts began to express themselves in spontaneous remarks. One day I got out of a long shower and said to my girlfriend, "I think I'm immortal," for it seemed clear that this body could die and yet I could not. I felt so odd at work that I began to worry my coworkers would think I was on drugs. Everything seemed still, dream-like, in some indefinable way. People came and went, scenes changed, days passed, and I was just watching it all happen, unconcerned, completely indifferent.

In the midst of all this, I was busy administering state tests and working on my game project. It was April in the Cascades, and the weather was beautiful. I was going out for lunch when I could. I would grab a sandwich and head up to a park on the banks of a river that flowed by the outskirts of town. And there, one day, it just happened!

I was eating my sandwich at a picnic table. The river flowed by some twenty feet down the embankment, across a grassy clearing. A cedar tree towered overhead. I watched a crow as I ate. She perched at the far edge of the long table. Others swooped in and landed on the ground nearby. I remember thinking how strange they looked, how familiar and yet how strange. I finished my sandwich, threw out my trash, and looked up at the trees —

I looked up at trees … and it was like the whole universe turned inside-out. That's the best description I've been able to come up with. There was a kind of optical shift, as if I passed through a tunnel, and then there was no inside or outside anymore. And I suddenly realized, all at once, like a voice echoing through all creation: *This is everything, absolutely everything! Everything that ever was, is, or will be is right here in front of me!* And it had been there all along. Time had fallen away into unreality, and everything in this eternal moment radiated with a brilliance that was shocking to behold.

No words can describe my amazement, my elation, my absolute joy. I couldn't believe what was happening, but it *was* happening! I took a few steps down toward the river, turned around in a circle, and laughed out loud. I laughed and laughed and laughed. It was all clear now, so absolutely incredible, and yet obvious. Though I could see everything as before, there was no separation between things. There was no near or far, and everywhere I looked, wherever my gaze fell, I recognized it all as nothing other than myself. The whole of creation lay before me, and I was it!

As I walked toward the river, I glanced behind me. I was so giddy with delight, so overwhelmed, that I thought my behavior might seem odd to anybody looking on. And while I had the strange sensation that somebody was watching from behind, it also seemed that someone was me. In any case, nobody was there.

Standing on the river's bank, I looked out over the rushing water, the still rocks, and the green trees. Clouds drifted in a clear blue sky. The world appeared at once the same and completely transformed. Everything was filled with sublime beauty, an astonishing radiance that could only be described as divine. And for a while, I just stood in awe.

And yet, this was the everyday world, the world we are already in. I glanced at my watch, remembering I had to be back at work soon. I looked across the river once more, somehow knowing it would be all right, that this wondrous vision would not vanish, and I headed back to my car.

The sensations I was experiencing were so new, so palpably different and disorienting that I didn't even know if I could drive. I got into the car and for a moment just stared at the controls. Then I told myself to be very careful, and I started the engine.

The school was not far off, and I got back without issue. The students were already in class, and I wandered the halls looking at everything, confirming in each thing I saw that yes, *I am that … I am that … and I am that too.* It's difficult to describe how incredible and yet how self-evident this is, that what we're seeing is our own being.

Despite all this, I found I could function completely normally. I spoke to students, administered tests, and talked with teachers. The rest of the day passed in utter amazement. And as I drove home that evening, down the long winding road through the mountains, the trees swayed with mysterious intelligence. Every dark corner of my being filled with bliss, and as the beauty of the world flowed around me, I knew my life had changed forever.

❧

I would have thought enlightenment to be more like understanding something and less like being wrapped in a blanket the size of the universe. Yet there I was, swaddled in the cosmos, with no way to account for it. There was no way to understand it with thoughts, just as there is no way to put it into words. I could only surrender, deeper and deeper, until there was nothing left of me. Had there ever been anything at all? Now there was only this awareness, and the ebb and flow of bliss.

It couldn't last though, right? I mean, I was going to go to sleep and wake up and everything would be back to normal. I would be myself again. How could I not? But that's not what happened. The next day I woke up and looked out the window. A light rain was falling, and I thought, *Oh, I'm raining,* and I realized the whole incredible happening was still happening. And seemingly overnight, all my usual troubling thoughts — my depression, my self-critical ideas, my fear and dread, my self-aggrandizing ambitions — were simply gone. My troubles were over. My search was over! It was a relief beyond imagination. Everything was present in this moment. There was nothing to seek. I couldn't imagine anything other than everything, and it was all right there.

In the weeks that followed, it's difficult to remember exactly when everything happened, because time had disappeared. The past and the future no longer seemed real to me. I was an unbound awareness, existing in an ever-present now. I cannot begin to tell you how astounding this is, and I considered a lot of things to try and explain my condition. Maybe I had a brain tumor? Maybe I was going crazy? One day I thought maybe I had died — really died. That's how radically different things were. For a few seconds I got caught in the thought. I tried to think when it could have happened. How did I die? How did my parents find out? I started to get really scared, until I realized these were only thoughts, and instantly they became transparent. I had only scared myself. I didn't have any symptoms of a brain tumor — no headaches, no motor control issues. I was perfectly rational, considering the circumstances. But most clearly, thoughts were only thoughts, and nothing more.

For a while I kept thinking that it must end. Somehow it would end, or I would mess it up. I would get into an argument with my girlfriend, or get frustrated with some student's behavior at work, or get wrapped up in a bunch of writing. And I would think, surely that will be the end of it. But nothing stuck — no thought that came up, no emotion that arose, no event that unfolded. When I tried to look inward, toward that inner life that used to seem so real, that place where all the thoughts and emotions used to accumulate, I couldn't find anything. There was nothing there. There was no me to mess it up, and I couldn't break reality, even if I tried. It's just what is.

I returned to the park many times, and surrounded by nature, I marveled at the beauty of the world. I gaped in awe. I wept with joy. I stood dumbfounded before the altar at the edge of infinity.

One day, the river was shrouded in mist. A goose appeared out of the clouds, flying upstream. It flew between the overhanging trees, low over the rushing water, and disappeared in the mist. Beyond the far bank some clouds cleared, and I watched the trees in the forest. A breeze blew, and something moved amidst the swaying of the high branches. I sensed something … something so beautiful … so overwhelming that I almost fell down. Tears streamed down my face. It was just … unbearable bliss and beauty.

It was beyond bliss, beyond indescribable, beyond beyond. And that, whatever you care to call it, is ever-present, here and now.

One day, I stood by the river and followed the fluttering flight of a butterfly as it made its way across the sunny clearing. Seized by a spontaneous impulse, I ran back along the bank and up a slope to a footbridge that led across the river. I felt like a child again, bursting with the joy of running. I ran out onto the bridge. I ran and ran. The far shore grew larger. The river raged beneath me. And suddenly it seemed I was not only crossing from one bank to another, but I was crossing into another world, a world beyond death. I kept running and running. On the far bank I walked up a boulder-strewn hillside, and there, I lay down on a large mossy rock, amidst wildflowers and tall grasses. I literally felt I was in heaven. *We've been here all along,* I thought. *Heaven is here and now. We just never noticed.*

As I walked back across the bridge, I stopped in the middle. I stood at the rail and looked downstream. All my life was flowing away from me. I looked down into the roaring river, where the swift water collected into a deep pool. I felt so complete that I thought, *I could jump into this river right now and die happy ... just disappear into bliss.* There was, of course, no point in doing it. This is a world without end. There is no real death. But somehow I knew that my life, the life I had been living, was finished. It had been a wonderful and adventurous life, but that person's life was over. And moved by that which moves everything, I turned from the edge and went on my way.

Words Words Words

Accounts of awakening invariably focus on the experiences that accompanied awakening, and yet, enlightenment itself is not transitory. It is not an experience that comes and goes, so even the best descriptions of the experience cannot paint the full picture. Such descriptions have value in that they may point others toward the possibility of awakening and encourage them on the path. But the actuality of enlightenment is literally ineffable, and so it makes sense to talk a little about the limitation of words, language, symbols, and by extension, symbolic and conceptual thought.

I am not a philosopher, or at this point in my life even a dedicated scholar, so please forgive any mistakes I make and try to cut to the very heart of what I'm saying. In any case, every argument comes with holes included; exhaustive detail only makes them less apparent. Language is a tricky thing, and doubly so when you use it to talk about itself or anything beyond its limits.

It is perhaps easily seen that a word is an abstract symbolic way of representing something in language. The word *tree,* for example, represents a tree. No problem. But it is more difficult to see that the word also defines the thing — delineates and separates it from everything else — and that naming happens simultaneously with conceptualization. Now we have a symbolic image of a tree as a thing. But those delineations, those separations, those boundaries of what is and isn't a tree, and where a tree ends and the forest begins, or where a forest ends and the rest of the world begins, are ultimately arbitrary. It may not seem like it, but our conceptual image is an imaginary thing. Strictly speaking, there are no things in the world. There are no trees. The same could be said of events, which are just another type of thing. A thing is just a conceptual unit of language, useful, but without any reality of its own.

So when you see a tree, consider that what you see is not a tree at all. A tree is a word, a symbol, a concept. What lies before you is a process, a form, or a feature of the unfolding universe. Its actuality is beyond all words. It is simply what it is, undefined, without limits. Its beginnings go back much further than a seed, and its ends are unknown. It is intimately interwoven with the soil and the sun, such that it cannot be separated from them. Who can say where it ends? And who can say what it is?

All words are like this. So when a word like *God* is used, it's all too easy to misconstrue the meaning. Such a word is heavy with conceptual, historical, and cultural significance that almost always obscures the truth it attempts to convey. Likewise, words like *delusion* or *conditioning* could seem very negative, even off-putting, but they are useful words when talking about a certain situation that exists within a larger context. When engaged with any words, it's important not to turn them into self-deceptions resting on preconceived ideas and the emotional reactions they provoke, but rather seek to encounter the ineffable to which all words ultimately refer.

Similarly, the very grammatical structures of language affect how we conceptualize the world. In English, for example, a verb has to have a subject, either explicitly or implicitly. Because of this, it's difficult for English language speakers to imagine something happening without also imagining something that's doing it. It's difficult to imagine thinking, for example, without also imagining someone who is thinking the thoughts. But if you observe your thoughts very closely, you'll see that they appear out of nowhere. Suddenly a thought is present. After some time it disappears again, as if into nothing. Is there someone thinking these thoughts, or is that person just a function of linguistic conceptualization? To most people, it no doubt seems someone is thinking, but is it true? Who is that person?

This is all to say that language and symbolic thought in general are not just descriptive and representative. They shape perception, perhaps to a far greater degree than we generally acknowledge or realize. Requiring words, language can only say something about that which can be defined. After a while, we tend to think that these discrete things and their defined attributes and interactions constitute reality itself. This being the case, perception and thoughts are limited accordingly. People are, in essence, perceiving not an objective reality, but rather a symbolic world, manipulated with symbolic thoughts and communicated through symbolic language.

With regard to using language, these difficulties are unavoidable. So don't get caught up in word games. Imagine for a moment that there is something words cannot touch, something which no symbol can represent, which no thought can grasp. This thing, which is not a thing at all, cannot be named. It cannot be named because to name is to define, to define is to limit, and it has no limits. Not only can it not be named, but nothing can be said about it. It's everything, but even that is saying too much, because it's also nothing. Any word you use will likewise create some such duality, and all dualities imply separation by mutual exclusivity.

Now imagine that this thing beyond all words, which again is not a thing at all, is the very foundation of reality itself. In this case, words may be helpful along the way, but they are only pointing, and rather vaguely at that. In writing I must resort to words and all their inherent ambiguities. That being so, I have no intention to nail down specific definitions and rigidly adhere to them as a philosopher might. I intend to write naturally, freely using available vocabularies.

The point here is that you should seek the truth yourself and not take anyone's word for it. Because ultimately, it is not this or that. If you want to know the truth, words and all the conceptual thoughts they imply, no matter how well crafted, will never get you there.

NIRVANA IS SAMSARA

Despite the trouble with words, there is no shortage of names for it. Some call it God or by the names of many varied gods and metaphysical concepts. Some call it Brahman or the Self. Others call it tathata, sunyata, or dharmakaya. Some call it Tao. And still others call it transcendental insight, consciousness itself, pure awareness, being, truth, or ultimate reality. Whatever you call it, and whatever philosophy, mythology, or metaphors you surround it with, it is the essence, the basis of what is, the very origin and ultimate end of everything. It transcends all thought, but at some point, obsessed with our thoughts, we become separated and lose sight of it. In a moment of fear and doubt, we exchange reality itself for our idea of reality, and we rarely go back in this lifetime.

The great myths speak of this. We are cast out of paradise, cut off from God. We are reborn into samsara, this world of birth and death, and find ourselves lost in our thoughts and delusions. In extraordinary moments, sometimes we may glimpse this ultimate reality, but do not realize it. And few recognize they *are* it, manifested briefly in this life, like a fleeting thought, barely grasped, like a flash of lightning or a shooting star. We build a wall of thought between ourselves and the reality of being. We separate ourselves with the idea of an inside and outside, of a self and other, of a mind and body. And this separation, this ignorance of our true nature, is the source of all our frustration and suffering, for we grasp at shadows and wisps of smoke, trying desperately to hold on to them.

Throughout history, mystics and yogis, great monks and sages, have attested to a way out. Many methods have been proposed: meditation and self-inquiry, devotion and renunciation, gurus and spirit guides, prayer and fasting, codes and mantras, pilgrimages and good deeds. A multitude of techniques have been devised, explained, and catalogued. Progressions, steps, and levels have been outlined and espoused endlessly. If one follows such a path, so be it, and if one makes it to the end even better, but in truth there is no path. The path itself is an illusion. There is no method, no technique, no way to get there. Each life is a puzzle, a labyrinth, a Gordian knot, that must be undone before awakening. But in the end, the puzzle itself will be smashed. The labyrinth will collapse. The Gordian knot will be cut clean through with the sword of truth.

I found my way seemingly by accident, and in a way maybe we all do, in so far as there are any accidents at all. In the end, all our efforts finally stop, and the truth reveals itself. I would have been the last one to admit all my problems were self-made, but they were. Despite being a writer of imaginative fiction, I never could have imagined this, and yet this is what's happening. I am now continually astonished by the appearance of world, directly perceiving its fleeting impermanence, its incredible beauty, its bliss and being, just as it is, arising in consciousness and passing away into nothing. I no longer identify with my former self. I simply recognize what is unfolding in this ever-present moment. My life continues, quite normally, but I am unbound from the grip of my thoughts and desires. Nothing can be gained or lost. The wind has stopped, but smoke from a blown-out candle still drifts in the air. What is this if not nirvana? I am free, and this very world of birth and death is shining with divine light.

THE BIGGEST SECRET

I felt as if I had discovered the biggest secret in the world, and in a way I had. There is no conspiracy that keeps us in ignorance though, no hidden knowledge that perpetuates our suffering. There are no forbidden texts withheld from which illumination might come, no lost land, sacred cave, or holy mountain where the answers lie. There is no guru or teacher who can save you. And there is no magical technique to unlock the mysteries of the universe. The truth is hidden in plain sight. It is right before you now, and you yourself have hidden it there.

How was it possible never to have seen this? It is the most extraordinary of all happenings. It is the greatest realization in all of life. Why wasn't everybody talking about this? Of course, I had myself as my answer. The fact is, some people *were* talking about it, but I had lost interest. I thought they were deluded, but I did not see the delusions of my own mind. I stood in the divine presence, but all I could see were my own thoughts and ideas. I had been lost in a world of illusions.

We are not our minds, or our bodies, or anything we can possibly think of. Our true nature is beyond all that. But at some point, we hid this from ourselves with thoughts. We identified with our minds, thoughts and memories, and with our bodies, actions and sensations. We created for ourselves a little island, an identity separate from everything else. Then it seemed we were like visitors to this world from somewhere else, but we couldn't imagine where. And this separation, between self and other, was the beginning of all the trouble and drama.

We hid our true nature in a web of illusions, and began to live through symbols and concepts. This process was so subtle, and yet so thorough, that we didn't even see it happening. And we kept this secret in the cleverest place imaginable: in the idea of a self. We tricked ourselves completely. We cannot know this secret without destroying the idea of ourselves. But who will destroy it? And who will know the secret when it is destroyed? And so we are trapped in a double bind. It is like we have hypnotized ourselves. It is like we are dreaming.

Everybody knows there is a lot of suffering in the world, from nagging everyday frustrations, anxieties, and unease, to overwhelming physical and psychological horrors. Depression and rage are common, and the world seems increasingly on the verge of disaster. Many people wish there was a way out. They look and look but nothing grants any lasting relief. Some seek power and wealth. Others seek pleasure and entertainment. Some seek drugs and oblivion. Others seek God and religion. Some seek knowledge and facts. Others seek spirituality and self-improvement. But nothing ends the endless struggle.

It's not all bad, but nevertheless, frustration, longing, and suffering persist. Eventually one might be inclined to think there is no way out. There is only the way through — through time, through the pain, through all the difficulties. And as long as one persists in this thinking, they are right. But there *is* a way out, and if you have ever reached this point of despair, you may be closer than you think. To get out, however, you must see absolutely that there is *no* way out, not only in life, but in birth and death too.

If you can look at the whole process and really see that there is absolutely nothing you can do about it, you have already let go. But you have to really see it, not just understand it intellectually. You must feel it to be so, and know directly, in the very core of being. There is no way to improve yourself. There is nothing to know. Nowhere to go. Nothing to achieve. Nothing to do.

When everything has been surrendered, the person you thought you were dies away. You step out of time, and suddenly realize there is nothing to escape from. The secret is revealed. It's all you, and there is nowhere but here and now. Enlightenment is real. You've been there all along. God is real, but beyond all imagination.

PART II

INSIGHTS

There is nothing
Else but this.
No self or other,
No past or future,
No inside or outside.
There is no explanation.
And yet …
No lack,
No need,
No want.

On Waking Up

I know how this all sounds to a skeptical mind. Before awakening, I would have described such accounts as sensationalist at best. But I am here to tell you that enlightenment is possible, even for a mixed-up person with no formal spiritual training, no long history of dedicated meditation, no exceptional virtue, and no real clue how to sort out the issues of life. Furthermore, although statistically rare and fraught with some genuine difficulties, awakening is closer than you think.

It is possible to reach the end of your problems. It is possible to unravel the mystery of life. It is possible to know the truth. It is possible to lose all fear of dying, all anxiety about the future, and all regret of the past. It is possible to live in this moment so completely that you see the world differently. It is possible to experience the oneness of everything as a permanent condition. It is possible, in a manner of speaking, to know God directly. But it all comes about in an unexpected way.

There is a kind of process at work, for lack of a better word, whose ends are unfathomable. In it all things unfold, and out of this process both delusion and awakening happen. The individual self cannot unravel it. And yet, this process is at work within you. In fact, everything that is *is* this process. And ultimately, your true self is not the individual self you have come to identify with, but a universal Self — or a no-self — which is one and the same with this process.

There is a price to be paid, though. You'll have to give up all your beliefs about who you are and about the world around you. That is not an easy thing to do. It turns out we hold on to many delusions much more deeply than even a fairly clear-headed person would suppose, so even identifying how far your beliefs go can be a challenge. In the end you must, in fact, give up yourself and everything else along with it. But for those who really long for the truth, no price is too high. And for those who are close to death, as all those living are in some sense, you have nothing to lose.

While we cannot take the final step ourselves, there are things we can do to bring us to the threshold. Spirituality itself can be a maze of delusions. But relatively speaking, there are deliberate actions an individual can take, ideas to consider, practices to undertake, and relentless inquiries to pursue, that may increase the probability of awakening, or accelerate the process. Therefore, books such as this, such accounts, such teachings, and such practices have a role to play.

Ultimately, my awakening was not by my own doing. It was more by my undoing than anything else, by the end of my self. So there is no pride of accomplishment, no claim of unique understanding or personal power. There is just deep gratitude, profound relief, and ever-present joy. Strictly speaking, there is nothing to attain, but my greatest wish is for you to attain this nothing, for you to feel this gratitude, this relief, this joy.

BEYOND ALL WORDS

I am going to discuss a variety of insights and ideas with their roots in a direct perception of something quite inexpressible. To some people these ideas may seem far-fetched, outlandish, even fantastical or delusional. To others the ideas may sound familiar, known, even old hat. But if this book is to be helpful for you, any reaction based in such judgments are a distraction. Please hold off on deciding anything, from believing or disbelieving. Instead, look to the emptiness between the lines, and to the unknowing space within yourself.

Because I must use words to convey such insights, it may seem as if I'm trying to convince you of something. I'm not. When it gets right down to it, I'm not even trying to tell you anything. In this way, I am not using words in the ordinary sense, to point toward things, ideas, and concepts, or to make an argument which you can then accept or reject. My purpose here is not to close the mind around a series of ideas and concepts one way or another, but to open it and point directly toward that which we are already.

The task requires both boldness and subtlety. I will constantly hint at that which can only be known directly. I cannot warn you strongly enough, not to mistake belief in any idea, concept, or story — old or new — for the truth. All such things are in the realm of thoughts, including the ideas presented here. But what I am pointing to lies beyond all words, beyond all ideas, beyond all thoughts.

At times I may say "You do this and that," or "You must do such and such." Please understand, this is just a way of speaking. I don't mean to make any assumption about you in particular. This is just a way of directly addressing our collective human nature and the mind in general. Consider these things carefully, as well as any reaction you may have to such statements. But of course, if you feel what I'm saying doesn't apply to you, don't take it personally.

Nevertheless, what I say may call into question core beliefs we hold about ourselves, the world, and our assumptions about life and reality. Depending on what beliefs one holds, how strongly they are clung to, and in what manner, readers may have a variety of reactions. A strong reaction can itself be an opportunity for inquiry and insight. *Why* did you have that reaction? What thought prompted that feeling?

It is impossible to say how any book or practice will affect us in the long run ... or how anything will affect us for that matter. Many experiences we have in life may not seem like they are leading us anywhere, or to have any immediate effect. But in the aggregate, such experiences can lead to awakening, quite beyond our own understanding. Some of the spiritual books I read when I was young and the experiences I had through practices were like planted seeds that came to fruition only years later. Some books I had not yet read were like bombs waiting to go off.

For example, twenty years ago, when I was living in New York, I bought a book called *Zen: Beyond All Words* by Wolfgang Kopp. It's a slim volume, which I proceeded to keep in my possession, year after year, without ever managing to read it. I started a few times, but always found the contents simple to the point of absurdity or even a bit condescending. And yet, I held onto the book. As it turns out, this was the book I read just prior to awakening. I tore through it, and the contents hit my mind like a sledgehammer.

So wherever you're at in your journey, make no assumptions. What's most important about these teachings is not the content, but what you, the reader, bring to them. If you truly understand yourself, you will understand everything. No text, no practice, no teaching can show you the secret, but all are an opportunity for inquiry, and through that the truth may suddenly be revealed.

ORIENTATION

The more I observe and talk to people, the more I realize we are all on a spiritual journey, whether we know it or not. And wherever you are is exactly the right place to be. If you're reading this book, I imagine that most of you are doing so because, like I was, you are looking for something — at the very least for some clues along the path you are on.

Before we go further, let's explore the idea of this spiritual journey. Where does it begin? Where does it end? How can one make progress along the way?

We can imagine this journey as one in which consciousness itself collapses into a particular point of view, identifies with a mind and body, and loses itself in a kind of dream, in a world of things, and in life and death. Once lost, sensing some lack, it tries to find itself. It looks everywhere but cannot find itself among the world of things. Until one day it just stops looking and, having never been absent, recognizes itself once more.

The journey is like an adventure into a labyrinth. Within we are confounded by mazes and locked doors, enticed by wondrous treasures, challenged by terrible monsters, and entranced by endless illusions. It can be great fun. But in the midst of the labyrinth, when things get bad, it can get very dark indeed. It can seem as if there is no way out. But when we have exhausted every possibility of escape, and all our efforts come to a grinding halt, it is possible to wake up as if in the midst of a dream, and realize the labyrinth itself — and everything in it — is not actually real in the way we had imagined.

This is the good news, and although the spiritual journey does not necessarily end there, it is important to say at least that much. It is possible to realize the enlightenment people throughout the ages have attested to. Whatever your true nature is, it already is, and cannot be apart from you. That means what you seek is already present. The kingdom of heaven is here and now. You have never been apart from it. Finding it is not a matter of reaching some distant place, but of realizing what is right in front of you.

This is where things get tricky, though. You can't simply wake yourself up, because the *you* who you think you are is part of the dream from which you seek to awake. It turns out you can't just will yourself to stop looking for a way out, either. No matter how hard you try, it just keeps happening. You're really wrapped up in it, and to stop you have to really stop.

This is a strange situation to be in. On the one hand, there's nothing we can do to force this change to come about. On the other hand, as long as we are searching, we must keep searching if we are ever to exhaust our efforts and really let go. So our search is not in vain; it just never succeeds in the way we imagine. The imagined path always fails, but when it fails completely, realization dawns in an unexpected way.

Ultimately, it's not as complicated as it sounds. It's quite simple. It's just a matter of letting go, but we must let go of all our desires and beliefs, our hopes and dreams, our fears and anxieties, our concepts, ideas, and opinions, and ultimately ourselves. The spiritual journey is one of true and total surrender.

While essentially simple, that may sound incredibly difficult, or even impossible, in the context of any person's life. However, even though it may be an ordeal to face and let go of all the things we are holding onto, to think that it must be terribly difficult or far off, or that such a journey is only possible for a select few, are just thoughts, and ones that can form obstacles to awakening.

Teachings, guidance, and practices can be helpful in this search. While such things cannot directly bring about enlightenment, they point toward awakening and plant the seeds of profound inquiry. Through such pursuits comes insight into unknowing, and through unknowing comes the grace of surrender.

There is no Problem

At some point in our development, we get a feeling or idea that there is something wrong. This can manifest in a variety of ways. Perhaps there is some kind of problem we feel we must solve, some question we feel needs answering, some knowledge we must gain, or some level of success we must achieve. We may feel there is some task to accomplish or some injustice that needs to be corrected. Or perhaps we just feel a general sense of wrongness, about ourselves, about the world, about life.

Some may deny the existence of this feeling, but we suspect there is something forced about their professed contentment. They are too sure of themselves, as if compensating with overconfidence for a hidden lack. When pressed, most of us will reveal an essential discomfort with the situation we find ourselves in. We tell ourselves it's just situational. In a way we are right, but it's not about any particular situation; it's about *the* situation. It goes right to the very heart of our existential awareness.

Much of what we do in life is by way of trying to address this feeling in various ways. But from where does the feeling or idea arise? And can it really be addressed by any of the things we are doing? Will working harder make us successful? Will more exercise make us healthy? Will a better diet make us live longer? Will a more harmonious relationship make us happy? Maybe — relatively speaking — but will any kind of self-improvement improve us fundamentally? Will any of it solve the feeling that is at the core of our discontent? Will any of it alleviate our existential dread?

It's not bad to work hard, exercise, and eat right, or to be a kind and caring person, or to entertain spiritual ideas. These are all good things that can be part of a balanced life. But they are not really going solve the greater issue. Nor will they relieve any nagging feeling that something is not quite right, that we have not yet arrived, not yet made it. So what is the solution? More exercise? A stricter diet? A new spiritual idea or religion? Perhaps a new car or a better-fitting jacket?

The curious thing about this feeling is that we can never quite pinpoint it. That's why our attempts at solving it are so often haphazard. We flail about in the darkness at phantoms and ghosts, entirely unaware that the problem is us. The feeling of unease or incompleteness arises from our belief in the thought-created boundary between ourselves and the universe. It is nothing other than our separation from the truth, our ignorance of reality, our alienation from God, our exile from the primordial consciousness that lies at the heart of being.

The solution lies not in going forward, ever searching for the answer. No superficial solution will work, and even the deepest, most serious thinking along these lines will only yield more questions. Any solutions going forward in this way can only ever mask the underlying issue or reveal the limitations of such thought. That is because, essentially, there is no problem. We have only forgotten that we created the problem to begin with, by drawing the distinction between ourselves and everything else.

We pretended to be separate and then proposed there was a problem to be solved other than our own imagined separation.

So the solution is not to take yet another step forward, but to take a step back, to an awareness that exists prior to distinctions. Step back and see as you once did, before there was any feeling that something was wrong, before any idea of yourself as separate and distinct from the world, before any notion of the known and unknown. Step back into consciousness as it is before you claim it as your own, and you will step into a timeless perfection. You will see clearly then that there is no problem. There never was.

The Illusion of the Self

There are two ways a person might attempt to rid themselves of all their supposed problems, whatever they may be. One way is to enumerate them, then unpack each one and figure out exactly how it works so you can fix it. The trouble with this method is that while you go through this process to resolve one set of problems, a whole new set of problems is being created. You'll never see the end of it. The other way is just to get rid of your self, not by dying, but by realizing that the self you identify with is a thought-created illusion. See this fully, and you will see that all our problems are only our problems when we treat this illusion as a reality. However, this does present its own difficulties.

Who or what are you, really? That's an interesting question. The answer may initially seem self-evident. Yet when pressed, many people elicit no more meaningful response than a name or simply "I'm me." One might say, "I'm a person," but what is that? All such answers are really evading the question. We have a sense of identity, of being somebody: a thinker of thoughts, a decider between choices, a doer of actions, a feeler of feelings, a possessor of traits. But where does that sense come from? It has been with us for so long that we tend to take it for granted. If you really dive into this question, though, you may discover some very interesting things. You may find there is no such self, and that you are without limits.

We can call the sense of self the ego. I would say the basic sense of self goes back even farther than the ego, but it really makes no difference what we call it. It is the persona with which a person generally identifies. It is the feeling of being *me*. It is the thing to which we attribute thoughts and emotions, and to which we attach all our ambitions and problems, hopes and fears, memories and dreams. Most people think of this ego as being somehow contained within the body, although not necessarily *of* the body. The ego is imagined, perhaps, as a kind of person inside the person, who is in charge of various volitional processes, and who possesses various automatic processes.

With a series of memories, a person constructs the image of a whole continuous life story and thinks, *This is my story; this is who I am.* But memory, ever in the present, can only ever be about the past. Memory can never tell us anything about this present moment, including who we are now, which is where we actually exist. We must then be who is having this memory. Surely that is who we are. But if we examine this present moment, we notice the memories seem to arise from nowhere, and we cannot predict what the next one will be.

In fact, there is no person inside your head, conjuring thoughts or making memories appear, or telling your hands to move when you write, or your legs to move when you walk. You will never find such a person. It is a fantasy, an imaginary entity created to fulfill various linguistic and social functions. There are only thoughts. There are just feelings. They only seem to be our thoughts when we imagine someone must be thinking in order for there to *be* thoughts. And every once in a while we have a thought that says, *These are my thoughts.* When these thoughts repeat enough, with a high enough frequency, it seems like someone is really there. But the ego is just a shadow of circumstance. Shine a bright enough light on it, and it will disappear.

From the very beginning of our lives, long before we even learn to speak, people are telling us who and what we are. You are this or that type of person. This is your foot; that is your hand. You like this; you don't like that. And so on. We grow up hearing these things, and the more we hear them the more real they become to us. Along the way we develop language, preferences, and memories. And we begin to tell ourselves and others who we are as well. *I want this. I want that. I saw this movie. I read that book.* Because a verb requires a subject, there is always this "I." And bit by bit we begin to identify with this "I," the feeling of it, and its life story.

One day, when we are still quite young, we realize this person we more and more clearly imagine ourselves to be, will one day cease to be. In that moment the ego is truly born. I remember clearly the moment I first realized I was going to die. It was a thunderous, overwhelming realization, and the knowledge of any interval of time before it happened, no matter how large, made no difference. I was going to die! In such a moment, the ego crystallizes into something that seems absolutely real. And suddenly, locked in this duality of existing or not-existing, we are already searching for a way out.

At the time, we cannot see the ego as an imaginary entity, because in the moment it is born we have already identified with it. It is the ego itself, in coming into being, that recognizes its own mortality. In that moment, all our problems have their root. From that moment onward, all our thoughts, emotions, and memories are attributed to this new found self, and all our troubles begin to accumulate around it. Eventually we may notice something is missing from our lives, and so the search begins. Many people speak of wanting to find themselves, but what are they really searching for?

Most people so thoroughly identify with the ego that it seems impossible to let it go. Some will reject the very thought that their idea of themselves may be an illusion. It challenges every notion they have about themselves, and the thought of letting go of it seems like self-annihilation or insanity. Others, hearing they must rid themselves of their ego to advance spiritually, desire to be rid of it. But they soon find that very desire to be sustaining it. From the start, the ego is constructed in such a way as to perpetuate itself.

It will confuse any attempt to see through it, and co-opt any attempt to get rid of it.

If you wish to truly see through this illusion, there are no easy answers. Try first to intellectually understand how arbitrary and insubstantial the ego is — a kind of construct cobbled together from various thoughts, sensations, and memories. Try to feel where this sense of self comes from, how it originates, how it renews and sustains itself in your thoughts. Be absolutely honest with yourself. But remember, the ego will claim each thought as its own. Cultivate a sense of letting go of your identity, rather than holding on to it. Prepare yourself as if for death, but know that you cannot force the ego away. You cannot do anything about it. The ego itself must be ready to die.

If it does happen that you see through this thing completely, you may find yourself disoriented, without any apparent center. All your troubles may seem to fall away. Your thoughts and actions may seem to just happen, effortlessly, motivated by the same thing that is motivating everything around you. Alternately, it may seem as if you are controlling everything. You may search and search for this "I" that was such a familiar feeling inside yourself, but you will not find it. It was always an illusion. There is no inside or outside. And you may realize then, that it was only part of a much grander illusion.

THE ILLUSION OF THE WORLD

The suggestion that the world itself, the entire phenomenal universe, is in some way an illusion may go against every feeling and thought we have. This is a difficult notion to get across, and inevitably many people will get the wrong idea. They will try to think it through and conceptualize it, and that is the illusion itself at work. They may think I am somehow denying reality or proposing some kind of metaphysical model, but that is just not the case.

Nevertheless, the way we think about the world and the way it generally appears to us is not its true nature. We need not negate the world entirely, but we should not mistake any concept we may hold about it *as* reality. Rather, what if we simply voided all concepts about it? All concepts are dependent on other concepts, so none can express the full reality that is before us. Even sophisticated ideas about reality have their roots in fundamental assumptions about discreet objects and events, with a separation between self and world.

Stripped of concepts, we are faced with our naked awareness and the inexplicable dance of reality unfolding within it. What else are we to conclude? There is no objective world. There is no subjective world. There is only this being, in which subject and object are one. Separation and all dualities are illusory, masking the deeper reality of transcendent being. Believing in the illusion or any part of it obscures the true nature of yourself, the universe, and the ultimate reality that permeates all existence and non-existence.

From very early on in life, when we started to make distinctions between this and that, we essentially took symbols and concepts as reality, and have been conditioned to believe in them ever since. But such symbols, such concepts, such things, are real only in the way a dream is real, for all distinctions are creations of the mind. And just as you can wake up within a dream and know you are dreaming, so it is possible to wake up in this life and know that this world is like a dream, whose multitude of forms lack any independent reality.

The world is an even deeper, more fundamental illusion than the illusion of the thought-created ego. This illusion encompasses the mind, time and space, and everything contained within them. It seems impossible to explain this, as our very thoughts will get in the way of understanding. Furthermore, the ego will resist anything that threatens its control over the mind, as any challenge to a conceptual basis of reality does. Therefore, it is highly likely that until you can see completely through the illusion of the ego, you will continue to take some illusion of the world as real.

This illusion is mistaken for a permanent reality by the thought-deluded mind, but it is more like a weaving of smoke. It is ephemeral, impermanent, and ever changing. While this may be understood intellectually, when the veil of illusion is actually lifted, the undeluded mind sees all forms just as they are, with all their impermanence, as manifestations of the ultimate reality.

This seemingly radical idea may sound plausible or implausible, and you may believe or not believe what I'm saying, but that is all beside the point. Those are just different ways of further deluding ourselves. Ultimately, one way or another, we must see through all that. The personal identity, its thoughts and beliefs, are all a part of the illusion. Our true nature and the true nature of the world is this undivided, ultimate reality I speak of. There really is no difference at all, but we must wake up to realize it.

TOTAL PERCEPTION

Perception is not a dead-end street running into the cul-de-sac of the self. It is more like a Möbius strip. With a mysterious twist it circles around, and when you finally make the whole circuit you see what's going on. You're right back where you started, and you realize there is only one side to the thing. Then the whole process becomes clear, and a kind of total perception unfolds before you.

It is widely believed that there is an external world and an internal mind or consciousness that is somehow aware of it. But where is this mind that is aware, if not *in* the world? And where is this world it is aware of, if not in the mind? No matter how you work it out, there is something very strange going on here.

It is only the creation of an internal ego identity and various conceptual models of an external world that prevent us from completing the full circuit. This makes perception look like a dead-end that ends within the self. This makes it seem as if *we* are perceiving *things*. But remove these conceptual roadblocks, and world perceives world, mind perceives mind.

Just consider for a moment that everything you see before you, every sound you hear, every sensation you feel, not to mention every thought and emotion, is happening in this phenomenon we call consciousness. There is no way out of it. It is the screen upon which everything is played. Because the screen itself is blank and we do not know what consciousness is, we tend to ignore it, and go about our business of seeing and hearing, sensing and measuring, and building various conceptual models to explain it all.

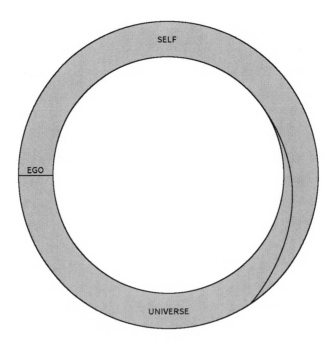

Consider the following model. A luminous object sits in space and is observed by a person. Light goes into the eyes and information is relayed to the brain via the optic nerves. The brain then creates an image which it projects in the consciousness of the observer. That's all well and good until we ask the following question: where is that image the brain is projecting, if not right in front of the eyes? It is an image complete with luminous objects, people, eyes, optic nerves, and brains. The image projected is the image perceived. There is no other image! And any imagined world beyond this image is pure fantasy.

I'm sure somebody could point out some scientific flaws in this model. For example, one could show a delay between an external event and an internal image. But that is missing the point. Anything you add, such as a brain delay, is also a part of the image. Again, there is only one image. You can't get out of it. You can go into these things in great detail, presupposing a variety of conceptual models and introducing ever-increasing levels of observation and accuracy, but you will never get to the bottom of it. Because there is no bottom! All conceptual models depend on other conceptual models. Once you start to construct one, you are already lost in thought.

The world is not physical. It is not mental. It is not spiritual. It is not temporal. It is not spatial. It is not causal. All such concepts attempt to stop the process of total awareness, to describe or fix it, in order to account for other dependent concepts, especially the ego. As soon as we set down that path, we are again lost in a world of thought and illusion. To find our way out, we must see everything, totally, all at once, without placing any thoughts, concepts, or conditions upon it.

With this total perception, you will see everything as it is and realize fully that what is perceived *is* that which is perceiving. Like the serpent that devours its own tail, subject and object are one and the same reality.

No Time but Now

We often hear sayings like "Live in the moment" and "Inhabit the present," but in my experience we've been doing it wrong. In one sense, there is no other place to be. Everything that exists is in this present moment, here and now. Everything that has ever happened has happened in the present, and everything that ever will happen will also happen in the present. There is no other time. However, we fill up this moment by projecting ourselves into various memories of a past or predictions of a future. We do it so thoroughly, so constantly, that we do not even really see the present moment. We see only our temporal projections.

When we imagine that the past and the future are real in some way, we are believing in an illusion, a projection of the mind. Both past and future are imaginary. Nobody has ever seen the past. Nobody has ever experienced the future. Even if you had some kind of time machine, wherever you went would still be now. This present now is all that ever was or will be. Yet for most of us the past and the future seem more real than the present. We tend to think about the present only as a function of the past and future, as a dividing line between the two.

By believing in the illusion of time, we create all kinds of problems for ourselves. In fact, all problems are time bound — all worries, all regrets, all causation, all blame, all guilt, all fear, and so on. All are dependent on the illusion of a past and future. The ego-self, as a construct composed of thoughts, memories, and predictions, is also bound in time. It cannot exist when awareness abides in the full light of the present moment. It vanishes like a ghost at dawn, along with all the problems, pain, suffering, and negative thoughts that have attached to it. So ask yourself: In this very moment, who are you? Right now, what problems really exist?

Another common assumption is that the present comes out of the past and proceeds into the future. While this may be a useful thought, a simple examination of our experience should be enough to see it is a mistake. Again, the present moment is all there ever is. It does not come from a past nor proceed into a future. Past and future are always imagined in the present. Examine your memories and thoughts of the future. Look closely and you will discover they are always happening now. The past is just a projection of present memory. The future is a projection of present predictions. Our entire sense of time is an illusion. There is only now.

Even to say there is a now can be misleading, although much less than saying there is a past and future. This is simply because *now* is a temporal concept, and might lead one again to believe in the illusion of time. So let us say, there is only *this,* that which is before you. It has no name. Although its forms are ever changing, it is eternal.

Not This Not That

Opposites always imply each other. We cannot have one without the other, because contrast is what makes the world intelligible. We cannot have black without white. We cannot have up without down, nor inside without outside. We cannot have positive without negative. And we cannot have life without death. We cannot have self without other, and we cannot have existence without non-existence. All opposites arise mutually, as if they are two sides of the same thing.

This unity between opposites is very difficult to talk about, because concepts and language are structured in such a way as to create contrast between ideas and things. We describe a thing by saying "It is this and not that," and hence all the conceptual, philosophical, and metaphysical arguments that go on and on and on. Is the world material or immaterial? Is there a soul or no-soul? Is there God or no God? Is there something or nothing? And if there is something, how is it that something came out of nothing? When really, it should be clear that something and nothing must arise mutually.

So beneath the surface of opposites, we find an underlying unity. We cannot really call it everything, since everything and nothing are unified within it. We cannot really call it oneness, because that would imply it is neither none nor many. We could call it nondual, but even that suggests duality. So whatever term we use, it must be used in a special sense that indicates it is without opposite. It is not this and it is not that. It is not a thing, and it is not nothing. It is not manifested or unmanifested. It cannot be conceptualized. It cannot even really be named. That is one reason why it has so many names. But it is beyond all that.

Some might say "That's just a bunch of word games." To which I would say "Yes, that's precisely the point! Why not put a stop to all the word games and just see the truth directly?" To do so, we cannot choose between this and that. We must abide in a *choiceless* awareness. We must dwell in this present moment, and simply see what's really happening, without conceptualizing it in any way. Do not try to put it into words. Do not try to make sense of it. And do not try to save yourself within it.

Why do we resist? In the realm of what is, there are no obstructions. There are no real conflicts, just as there are no real opposites. But our very sense of self is caught up in the game of opposites. We feel that in order to exist and not lose our minds, we must identify with this or that thing or idea or concept. And every thought we make real, every concept we believe in, blinds us from the truth. This is the real meaning behind the gospel saying that "whoever would save his life will lose it." There is a certain letting go of knowing anything that must happen before the truth can be known. But whoever knows this truth will be free.

There is Nothing to Hold

I'm going to tell you something that may sound disappointing, at least at first. Some of you may even find it a disturbing or scary idea. But once it is realized through and through, it's the most wonderful thing. This is it: there is nothing to hang on to. Let me say that again. In this whole universe, there is absolutely nothing you can hang on to. Even this idea cannot be clung to.

No possession, no idea, no ideology, no concept, no belief, no inner state or experience, no outer circumstance, no relationship, no person, absolutely nothing will hold up. It may seem as if you can cling to this or that, but if you really look closely you'll find it has no substance beyond a temporary, relative sense. As a Zen saying puts it, you cannot nail a spike in the sky. And it's all sky! It is all a weaving of smoke, through and through. Anything you can possibly think of to explain it all or describe it is already an illusion. Any attempt to grasp hold of it and you will instantly lose it.

All things, including ideas, concepts, et cetera, are relative. That is just the nature of things. You may choose one or another thing to believe in, but it will not hold up to the absolute. All things exist only in relation to other things. Various things may be true in the relative sense, but that's just because things are set up that way. If things were set up a different way, it would no longer be true. Furthermore, all things are impermanent. Nothing lasts. The most cherished thought comes and goes. The highest mountains will crumble to dust. The stars themselves will eventually go out. Everything that is passes away into nothing.

Almost everyone has things they are clinging to, especially ideas. Some of them may be very obvious, while others may be so subtle, or so taken for granted, that you are unaware of what they are. Examine everything you believe, every idea or presupposition you have when making a decision or thinking about anything. Get right down to the bottom of it and ask yourself: what can you really say for certain?

Most of us believe in something because we are looking for some stable position upon which to base our life and thoughts. We're looking to ground ourselves, our feelings, or our ideas. We are looking for some sense of security, for some safety in a seemingly dangerous and chaotic world. But if you look deep, with absolute courage and honesty, you will see there is no ground and there is no center … at least none that you do not create.

This kind of talk makes some people very uneasy. If I say "There is absolutely no security, no safety to be found anywhere, and any attempt to grasp for it is a delusion which will create suffering," some people are not going be very satisfied with that. They might ask "What do you hold on to then?" To which I would say "Why do you feel you need to hold on to something?" They might say "What purpose does life have then?" To which I would say "Why do you feel life needs a purpose?" They might declare "That's just nihilism." To which I would say "Why cling to such a negative idea?"

It all comes back to our attachments. An inquiry like this could go on and on. In fact, these types of questions and answers form a large part of some spiritual paths. The basic idea is to root out and demolish every position the student may cling to, every idea upon which they may try to base some concept or argument. If this goes on long enough, the student may begin to realize the futility of taking any position. Even longer, and the student may finally stop grasping. At that moment there is a chance to see through it all and realize enlightenment.

What then? Well, then you will see how wonderful it is to have absolutely nothing to hold on to. Because when you really see that there is nothing you can grasp hold of, and you let go of everything you were trying to cling to, you are free. And in that unbound freedom, that absolute openness, when the fire of your thoughts and desires has blown out, you will discover there is no need to search for security. You will be, as it were, in the arms of God, as you always have been. And in that is a kind of security undreamt of. You can never hold onto it, but nevertheless it's holding you.

Hope is more
Tenacious than Fear

Some six months before my awakening, I made a strange gesture toward letting go of all hope and fear in my life. At the time, I was very interested in the work of Alejandro Jodorowsky, and was reading his book on *Psychomagic*. Inspired by the premise that symbolic acts could have real effects on the subconscious mind,

I decided to commit such an act. It was pure whimsy. I had no expectation of anything happening, and looking back the whole episode seems intensely like a dream.

I climbed to the top of a mountain. It was actually more of a butte just outside of town, but that was my holy mountain. While up there, I tore a 3x5 notecard in half. On one half of the card I wrote *HOPE,* and on the other half I wrote *FEAR.* I put the hope card under the heel of the insole in my right shoe, and I put the fear card under the heel of the insole in my left shoe, with the idea that I would be stomping these things out of my life. I said to myself, "I will know when to take these out." Then I put my shoes back on, went down the mountain, and went about my life.

I laugh even now when I think of this story. I never expected it to come about, let alone to come about in such a dramatic and complete way. But it seems that's exactly what happened. One day, several months after my awakening, I was telling this story to a friend as I was getting ready to leave her house. Suddenly, I took my shoes off again to show her the cards. "Look," I said, pulling up the insoles of my shoes. We looked inside, but there was nothing left except a few flakes of tattered paper. Both hope and fear had disintegrated under my heels. It was the perfect ending to my story.

Now, why had I done that? Why did I want to rid myself of hope and fear? I'll go into it in more detail, but simply put, these things create a lot of frustration, pain, and suffering. On some level I realized hope and fear were somehow fundamental to all the problems in my life. And I would suggest it's probably true in most people's lives. So let's go into it a little.

Let's start with fear, because most people can easily see how fear causes problems for them. You may think about something terrible happening and fear rises up within you. You experience all kinds of worry, anxiety, and psychological and physical tension on account of it. None of this does one bit to stop the terrible thing from happening, and you go through it all, whether the thing happens or not. Furthermore, fear tends to feed upon itself. The more fear is operating in your life, the more you experience it, even over minor things.

You might argue that fear has some benefits. How would we learn from the past if we had no fear of repeating our mistakes? When you were young, for example, you may have gotten burned and now your fear of fire keeps you from putting your hand in a flame. But that is not really fear. Unless you have a phobia or past trauma resulting in a psychological fear of fire, you are not really afraid of fire. You simply know that if you put your hand in the flame you will get burned, and you would rather not get burned so you don't put your hand there. That's intelligence in action, not fear in the way I am using the word.

What about a case in which you accidentally put your hand on something hot, feel the burning, and suddenly move away. Is it fear that makes you move? Again, no. Moving away from a painful stimulus is simply a natural reaction. If the tea is too hot you take the cup from your lips without sipping. It is nothing more than this. The kind of fear I'm talking about arises from thinking, from imagining unpleasant outcomes.

How about a case in which you must undergo something painful either because it is inevitable or because it may have some other benefit? Okay, this is a situation in which fear can arise, especially if there is time to think about it. But again, the fear is psychological in nature. In this case it is a fear of pain. Whether the imagined pain is physical or psychological, ultimately the fear is thought created, a function of various projections into the past or future. In an emergency situation, if one acts immediately, without hesitation, there is no time for fear to arise. In this present moment, unbound by time, we are all absolutely fearless.

Now let's talk about hope, because here is where many people will have objections. How can you live without hope? Hope is what keeps us going. Hope is what makes life worth living. You have to have some hope! But do you really?

Hope is not what makes life worth living. Hope is what keeps us from really living our lives. Let me explain.

What is hope? It is the opposite of fear. You project yourself into the future, imagine something good, and desire it. Since opposites arise mutually, as long as you have hope in your heart, you will also have fear, since you will fear your hopes may not come to pass. But that is only the beginning of your problems.

In my life, I had hoped to become a successful writer. For many years, this was a powerful motivation for work. I worked and worked at writing, always hoping some day a big success would come. There's no doubt that hope can be a powerful motivator. But I was also constantly frustrated by circumstances. I had to pay the bills. I didn't have enough time. And I was afraid that I had somehow wasted my life and my chance for happiness, because there was good chance I would never be successful.

Hope is like the carrot you dangle in front of a mule. You project a happier version of yourself into the future, but no matter how far you go, your happiness is still out there ahead of you somewhere. You are hoping for something you imagine to be better than what is in this present moment. And once you become habituated to this way of living, you will always project something into the future to keep you going. If one hope is realized, you will immediately hope for something more. What else could you do? You have to have hope. But while you are fixated on this imagined future, you are missing the only thing that really matters, the only thing that really is, and that is what's happening now.

I think this explains how hope can cause frustration and suffering, but some of you may not be convinced. There is a positive aspect of hope that maybe I have not fully addressed. We may think the frustration, the suffering, and even fear are all worth it in order to hang on to this positive quality of hope.

But the thing is, there's something we don't yet see while still bound up in hopes and fears. And we *cannot* see it until we wake up from those thought-projected illusions. When that happens, when we really let go and there is no more hope to hang onto, suddenly we realize there is nothing missing. One feels no lack at all. Instead, everything is present. There is no need to hang on to hope. One's deepest hopes are here already.

Thought-Projected Experience

The usual experience is a thought-projected experience. To experience oneself as a separate "I" contained within a body, cut off and distinct from an outside world, moving through time between birth and death, is an experience created by the repetition of conditioned thoughts. Fixated on these thoughts and the particular experience they create, we ignore the spaces between them, always looking for the next self, world, and time-reaffirming thought. In this way, we become locked in the projected experience and blind to anything beyond it.

How do we cut through or collapse this conditioned experience? Maybe it will help to map out some of the thoughts that create this experience. Imagine a diagram with horizontal and vertical axes intersecting in the middle. The horizontal axis represents time, with past to the left and future to the right. The vertical axis represents space, with the self above and the world below. Around the whole thing draw a big circle, and around the intersection of the two lines draw a small circle.

This is, of course, a graphical representation of a conceptual model, so it's important to remember this is itself a thought experiment. If it helps you see things in a new way, great. But don't get too attached to the model. If it doesn't help you, that's fine too.

Let's start with the time axis. It seems obvious to say, but all thoughts about the past and future create a sense of time outside the present moment, which is where everything is always actually happening.

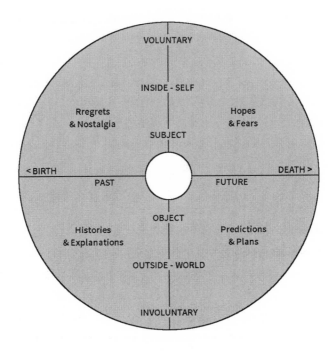

Through predictions we create a sense of a future. We imagine various things that might happen and, judging those things to be desirable or undesirable, we generate a wide variety of hopes and fears. Repetition of these thoughts creates a sense of anticipation and anxiety about the imagined future. This can happen on a far-reaching scale, imagining what will happen tomorrow, next week, next year, or in forty or fifty years. Or it can happen on a very small scale, in which we are, moment to moment, predicting and anticipating what will happen in the next moment.

Through memory we create a sense of a past. We imagine various things that have happened and, judging them good or bad, pleasant or painful, we experience various regrets and feelings of nostalgia. Regrets are a kind of fear that the past will affect the future, while nostalgia is a kind of hope that the past will return again. Repetition of these kinds of thoughts leads to more predictions, more hopes and fears, and an uninterrupted stream of desires and anxieties. In this way, the past is intimately connected with the future. They are, in fact, mutually arising opposites.

So that's time, an imagined past and future created by the projections of our present memories and predictions, our hopes and our fears. Into this realm of time, we also project the space containing our concepts of self and world. The top part of the vertical axis represents the self, imagined as everything that is internal and everything we do of your own control. The bottom part of the axis represents the world, or the other, imagined as everything that is external and happens outside of our control, right out to the ends of the cosmos. This axis also represents subject and object.

Back in the past, where the timeline intersects the large circle, that's birth. And out in the future, where it again intersects the large circle, that's death. Notice that in this diagram everything outside the big circle is simply outside of the projected experience. What is before birth and after death is united in sameness, as is everything that is beyond the self and the world.

Because the projections of time and space are intricately interconnected, collapsing one can collapse the other. But what's in the middle? What happens when you stop projecting thoughts into the past and future, into the self and world? We find that the very center is empty. It can be imagined as a kind of hole through the disk of projected thoughts. And when awareness collapses into that hole and passes through it, you are beyond birth and death, and beyond the separation between self and other. Suddenly you realize that the paper upon which the whole diagram is drawn *is* consciousness itself.

WORLD AS CONCEPT

However you conceive of the world, it is likely to be deeply embedded in your projected ideas about yourself, others, and the phenomena around you. The predominant world concept these days is that of a physical, material, mechanistic universe. This concept may be so deeply embedded in your thoughts that it is taken for granted as fundamentally real.

This idea of the world, though, is only that: a concept of what is and how things work. Our sensation of the world as a physical, material, mechanistic experience is a thought-projected experience. Again, it's easy to misconstrue all this as a simple negation of the physical world, but that's not the point. The point is that the world as it is conceptualized is different from the world just as it is. In the same way that the word *water* cannot quench your thirst, concepts of the world cannot satisfy our inmost feelings.

This is not about saying any particular concept of the world is right or wrong. We could just as easily conceive of the world some other way. For example, we could conceive of it as a mental construct, like a dream, in the mind of a god-like being. We could conceive of it as a simulation running in a giant supercomputer or an artifact created by alien gods. We could conceive of it as a vast self-generating organism. We could conceive of it as pure consciousness, or pure information, or pure energy.

The world is actually not any of these things. It is not physical. It is not mental. It is not spiritual. It is not mechanistic, logical, chaotic, dumb, energetic, or intelligent. These are all ideas you can grasp onto, but the world is not an idea. It is just as it is and nothing else. And yes, this may sound ridiculously simple. But the moment we start to conceptualize it, we are creating a symbolic projection based on an idea, lodged in our sense of self and other, past and future, and ten thousand other things. And as long as we abide in a conceptual paradigm of any kind, we will continue to be lost in the complexities of thought and illusion.

What would happen if you just looked at the world, seeing whatever came into your view, without conceptualizing it in any way? Could you do it, even for a moment? What would happen if you admitted to yourself that you really don't know anything, that you have no idea what's really going on, or even who or what you are? What would happen if you realized that there were no ultimately satisfying concepts of the world? What would happen if you saw yourself in an impossible situation in which there was no way out, no way of stopping it, no way of understanding it, and absolutely no way of doing anything about it? In that situation, what would happen if you just let go?

The Transparent Mind

Before awakening, the mind is a seemingly endless stream of obsessive thoughts. We cling to these thoughts and identify with them. We call them *our* thoughts, and we reaffirm our sense of self by believing them. After all, we are the thinker of our thoughts, right? If our thoughts are real in some sense, we also must be real.

Many people are so identified with their thoughts that the idea of looking beyond them to the consciousness in which they appear simply never occurs to them. Furthermore, because the ego-self references the continuity of these thoughts, they are ever grasping at the next one, whatever it is, to maintain this thought-based sense of self. And so they are constantly lost in streams of thought.

We are always getting caught up in believing various thoughts, often whether we want to or not. They seem so real to us. And because we get so mixed up in believing a whole host of negative, contradictory, and conflicting thoughts, many problems result, such as depression, anxiety, self-loathing, anger, and so on.

Soon we latch onto thoughts about those problems. They too get incorporated into the ego, and the problems themselves become part of our identity. Then come thoughts about our thoughts about our problems, and pretty soon we're in an incredible tangle. But it's *our* tangle, so we stick with it, hoping the next thought will sort it out.

Of course, there's no end to this. As long as we identify with and believe each thought that arises, we will be lost in thoughts. Our sense of self, which is itself a thought, becomes so hopelessly intertwined with memories, concepts, predictions, hopes and fears, that there seems to be no way of clearing the air. It's exhausting.

When we see that these thoughts are like wisps of smoke forming and vanishing in the clarity of consciousness, we are already close to the truth. There is no thinker of these thoughts, and no self to cling to them. They are only thoughts, appearing against a backdrop of pure consciousness. In meditation, many people can see this for themselves. But however it happens, prior to awakening, the process of continually identifying with our thoughts must come to an end.

After awakening, various thoughts still arise, but they are now transparent. There is no self to cling to them, and no ego to believe in them. When there is no attachment to thoughts and you can no longer believe in them the way you used to, there are no problems. The clarity of pure consciousness is seen through each thought that arises. And in the place of that former tangle of self-obsessive thoughts, there is timeless awareness without subject or object, the presence of an incredible and mysterious beauty, and the ebb and flow of bliss.

The Transparent Body

The feeling we have that we are in our bodies, contained somehow within our skin, is a habit created by social conditioning and a combination of mind activity, muscular tension, and various movements within the body. As we go through life, sensations, thoughts, emotions, and nerve impulses create patterns of tension and energy in the body. This creates an overall sensation pattern, which we then identify with. Identification with this pattern, in turn, creates more thoughts and emotions, deepening the sense that we are somehow in the body. You can work it out yourself by observing carefully your reactions to various sensations, thoughts, and emotions, and by identifying the unconscious patterns of tension and movement in the body.

Because of this, thoughts and emotions related to our experiences in life tend to become integrated into an ongoing pattern of muscular tension, and subsequently are incorporated into our sense of identity and self. We hold onto those emotions inside the body and identify with the feelings they create. This is why deep-rooted emotions can be brought up by certain types of massage. However, because we identify with the pattern of tension and the associated emotions, and because the various patterns have become interdependent, they can be very difficult to change or remove.

To a certain extent, that's all perfectly normal. Over time, however, patterns of chronic tension can lead to a variety of physical dysfunctions, decreased mobility, and health problems. The emotional traumas we hold on to can likewise become unbearable. And yet we find ourselves unable to let go of them. You end up like a person who is carrying around a boulder, but refuses to let go of it. The boulder has become a part of you. To lose it would feel like losing yourself. Who would you be without it? Anybody who has had an addiction may know this feeling. Well, the fact of the matter is, you're addicted to your self.

Working directly with the body and observing it, just like working with and observing the mind, not only has obvious health benefits, but can also lead to insights into our deeper identity. Such insights are possible at any time, but are perhaps more likely at the extremes of physical endurance, from exhaustion or pain, or from a wide spectrum of skilled physical work.

At the body's limits, or under the influence of intense interaction, the chronic patterns of muscular tension, along with the thoughts and emotions that support them, can be significantly changed. When the usual patterns of tension you identify with are diminished or altered, there is an opportunity to realize they are not you. In short, you are not your body or the feeling you have that you are inside it.

When this cycle of body identification ends altogether, and you wake up from this illusion of the self, you will not feel as if you are in your body, nor will you feel you are out of it. The feeling of self will be gone all together. There will be no inside or outside anymore. You may still have old patterns of tension residing in the body, but you will no longer identify with them. The body becomes continuous with everything around it, and you will realize that sensations, injuries and illnesses, aging and death, are part of the very process from which the universe unfolds. The body will be transparent. You will feel the winds of the cosmos blowing through it, and will know that wind and body are one.

Emotional Alchemy

The medieval subject of alchemy concerned itself with the search for a way to transmute base metals into gold. While this transmutation didn't really pan out in the modern science of chemistry, there is a metaphorical aspect to alchemy which is still relevant to discussions of spiritual transformation. Just as amorphous black carbon, when exposed to immense heat and pressure, can transform into a transparent diamond, so too can delusion and ignorance, when exposed to the light of awareness, be transformed into awakening and enlightenment.

Such transformations can be especially helpful when encountering a variety of negative thoughts and emotions — from anxiety, fear, and anger, to jealousy, greed, and regret. Even negative physical sensations such as discomfort and pain can be transformed this way. Whatever comes up can be transmuted through direct exposure to your conscious awareness.

Not long after my awakening, I had a dream in which my old feeling of rage reappeared. In the dream, I was painting a picture of a beautiful landscape. I was almost finished and very pleased with the result. While I was painting, somebody came in, took a brush and smeared it all over the canvas, completely messing up the painting. In that moment, rage appeared, welling up out of nowhere. But instead of being overwhelmed by it, I looked at it. I cannot describe it any other way ... I just gazed directly into my rage. And when I did, it transformed into absolute clarity.

There was no rage anymore. There was only clarity, but it was not clarity *of* anything — it was just pure clarity.

In the Tibetan Buddhist tradition, there is a system for purifying afflicted emotions which identifies a variety of negative emotions and the wisdom energies they transform into when seen for what they are. The system and the catalogue of emotions and energies is not important here. What's important is to understand and experience that such transformations are possible. If you can look directly at your negative emotions without identifying with them, you will see for yourself what they turn into.

When a negative emotion arises, either in response to a thought or environmental stimulus, do not fight it. Pushing it away or struggling with it only empowers the emotion and reinforces the ego to which it attaches. Instead, experience the emotion fully. Try to gaze directly into it. Observe your bodily sensations, such as where tension or pain accumulates, and any changes in breathing or heart rate. If you look at it with complete acceptance, experiencing it as pure sensation, you can actually watch it transform.

By looking directly at negative emotions and accepting them for what they are, you cease to identify with them. The emotion cannot attach to the ego, and a kind of space opens up in which the transformation can take place. The emotion becomes transparent, and the aspects of consciousness from which it arises shines through. You cannot will the transformation, however. That is just another way of resisting, of pushing away the emotion. Try to have no expectation or desire. The gaze itself is enough. Observe what's really happening and you will see base metals turn into gold.

Remember Where We're Heading

It's easy to feel lost and disoriented when we encounter these kinds of ideas. They don't always seem logical, and they are not aimed at the kind of knowledge that can be accumulated or understood in the way we're used to. It's tempting to feel like we have to somehow remember all this, and when we have insights or figure something out, it's tempting to feel like we have to figure it *all* out in a way that makes sense to our minds. But nothing could be further from the truth.

The purpose of this discussion is not to give you anything. In this journey, there is little point in accumulating the kind of knowledge you can memorize, categorize, integrate, or file away for some imagined future use. Remember, what we're talking about is always present, here and now, and fundamentally cannot be grasped or put into words. The purpose of this discussion is to help you realize *that* for yourself.

Transcendent wisdom is possible, but it cannot be conveyed or given to you. Your true nature is already your true nature. In this sense you are already enlightened; you just haven't realized it. The only way forward is by letting go of all the things that obscure this realization. Adding new things, however enticing, will only further obscure your vision. Instead, we must remove everything, as if taking off the garments of our imagined reality, until we stand naked before the truth.

So the purpose here is simply to point toward *that,* and to provoke inquiry into anything that lies in the way. As such, it is far better to ask questions than to come to conclusions. What does it mean to be attached to an idea, a belief, or a concept? What are you holding on to? Who is holding on? How can you let go? When it comes right down to it, what are you … really? Beyond what you've been told and what you think and believe, what is this experience that is happening? What is beyond all thought? What can you really say is true?

Don't be discouraged if you don't know the answers. Abide in unknowing. Do not dismiss the questions by fitting them into some conceptual system of understanding. Do not believe any readily available answer. Do not seek the safety of assurance, or to ground yourself in anything. We are going to a place where there is no ground.

There is no Explanation

When the truth is plain to see, no explanation is necessary. The truth requires neither proof nor belief, because it is that which, when found, is entirely self-evident. The final realization, however, simply cannot be explained. Why is that?

Explanations are tools of the mind, used to coordinate collections of concepts and symbols in such a way as to create some functionality, or to create new concepts and symbols. However, it is a big mistake to think that an explanation *is* reality, or that only what can be explained has any reality. Explanations can be used as a way of understanding and manipulating the world around us. But the ego uses the explanations to reinforce itself and other delusions, perpetuating any suffering those delusions create.

All explanations fragment what would otherwise be whole and indivisible. They separate one from the reality of what is. All explanations are limited and conceptual. The truth is unlimited and non-conceptual, and yet it can be known through total perception and awareness of being.

As we go through life, we frequently look for explanations that will fulfill us or solve our problems in some way. The ability to explain may indicate understanding, but what we understand is simply the explanation itself. We then make the mistake of equating the ability to explain with knowing, and even being. So it's no wonder we are constantly looking for a better explanation, or a more complete conceptual model.

I remember taking some university classes taught by brilliant professors whose lectures always left me feeling I was just about to grasp an explanation that would make everything clear. I thought, maybe at the end of the semester that clarity would come ... but it never did. The clarity of any explanation is strictly relative to the concepts involved. Go one step beyond and it is no longer relevant.

One might say I'm trying to explain things here, but the point of such an explanation is only a prompt to let go. Still, any explanation gives us something else to hang on to. In the end, we'll have to let go of that too. When we are silent, unknowing, reality shines forth and becomes clear. So why bother with any explanation? Well, some explanations may be helpful while fears or doubts remain, or when confusion is a larger obstacle than the explanation will be. But make no mistake: with an explanation we are at best exchanging one obstacle for another. If you can, foregoing any explanation, let go of everything now.

Whatever you think you know, imagine for a moment that it is all wrong. Imagine you have absolute assurance that every concept you hold, every explanation you grasp, is incorrect, inadequate, and insignificant. But there is nothing to replace your ideas with. Anything you've ever heard and anything you can think of is also wrong. After digesting this a little, turn your attention to what you are actually aware of, right in this moment. Now, what is it that you are experiencing? Resist the desire to latch on to any new explanations. They are wrong too! What is beyond all explanation?

No Need No Want

When you've spent half a lifetime desiring, it is indeed startling to suddenly have no desire. I spent a lot of time wanting things to be different than they were, and being frustrated by situations in my life. I wanted success, fame, happiness, love, understanding, sex, health, material pleasures, profound suffering, personal heroism, and spiritual fulfillment. I wanted more sleep too, and more time, less junk mail, fewer bills ... so many things I couldn't even name them all. I wanted to be everyone. I wanted to live every life.

I wanted to fall in love with every woman. And I was constantly frustrated by the feeling of some lack. Even when the objects of desire were present, there was always more desire. There was never any real end to it. And there never could be.

What is desire if not the feeling that you need something to fulfill you in some way? It is the feeling that out there, somewhere, there's something good, and if only you could get it you would be satisfied. If only you just worked a little harder. If only you would get that lucky break. But when you get a break, after a brief moment of satisfaction, you are already on to desiring the next break, or something better. There's always something more and better that could be achieved or hoped for, whether it is a better job, more recognition, a more fulfilling relationship, less pain, a longer life. It just goes on and on and on.

The ego is forever desiring things in search of a fulfillment it cannot achieve. The ego itself could be described as the desire to be somebody, some lasting separate entity. To justify its own self importance, it perpetuates more desires and attaches them to itself. Each additional desire gives the ego a reason to go on, always promising some future reward, some lasting happiness, some permanent satisfaction, should it ever get these things. But it will always want more, because if you suddenly found yourself with absolutely no desire, the illusion of the ego would vanish.

What you truly seek is beyond all desire, because you cannot desire that which is ever present. Nothing can fulfill you because you are already fulfilled. After awakening, this seems perfectly simple and obvious, but beforehand, nothing could seem more confusing and difficult to understand. That is the power of delusion and the mystery of enlightenment.

Eventually, when your search finally comes to an end, you are united with your true being. Then an enormous feeling of relief washes over you. There is nothing more to figure out — nothing to seek. Enjoyment of the present does not cease. In fact, you are enjoying the present and everything in it as you never have before. However, there is nothing more to want, no feeling of need, and no frustration of ongoing desires. You completely accept this moment as it is, and you are at peace.

CONTEMPLATING DEATH

From the moment we comprehend that death applies to us, it is a terror. Many people try to avoid thinking about it, seeing it, or even mentioning it — as well as simply trying to avoid it. Although this attitude of avoidance is very prevalent in Western culture, it is important to recognize that death is coming, sooner or later. No matter what the intervening time period, there is absolutely nothing you can do about it. And the chance to see this and accept it completely, before death actually comes, is a great opportunity.

I used to get nervous sometimes on plane flights, especially on takeoff, landing, or during bouts of turbulence. Whenever this would happen, instead of trying to avoid thinking about it, I would imagine the worst. I would really go into it, imagining the catastrophe unfolding, the plane plummeting through the air, the absolute certainty we were going to crash. I would imagine the horror and the screaming of the panic-stricken passengers as we tumbled toward the earth. I would imagine the moment of impact, the incredible forces ripping everything apart, the shock of terrible violence and pain, and then nothing … total annihilation. Somehow, when I really thought it all through, it didn't seem so bad, and I was no longer nervous.

If you have an extreme fear of flying, I don't necessarily recommend it on your next flight, but maybe you see the point. If you have any fear of death, ask yourself: what are you afraid of? Imagine it happening, and observe your thoughts and emotions closely. You may discover what you're really afraid of is not death, which is unknown to you, but rather something else, like pain, or leaving something undone, or leaving behind loved ones, or losing your life, or not having fully lived your life.

Over the years, I have had quite a few dreams about death, and a handful in which I died in the dream. One time, I drowned. Somehow I had been plunged deep into the water, with no hope of reaching the surface. I remember struggling and thinking I would die. I experienced a few frantic moments of pain and terror as I breathed water into my lungs. It was all very unpleasant, but then a deep peace came over me. I died … but awareness remained. I found myself looking at the silhouette of my body, as the light of a distant sun filtered through the turquoise water and radiated all around it.

In another dream, after death I encountered a kind of oceanic void, seething and frothing with an indescribable intelligence.

What can be said of such an encounter? I can barely convey it, but I've always counted these dreams a blessing. If you have the opportunity to experience death in a dream, do not be afraid to experience it fully. Follow it to the end and see where it goes. Go into it with complete acceptance, and see what happens.

Do not be afraid to think about death or to see it. Do not avoid the company of those who are dying or grieving. When I had a job answering questions for cancer patients and their families, I noticed that it was often the people who were worst off who seemed the happiest. You can draw your own conclusions from such observations, but it's worth contemplating.

Death implies life, just as life implies death. To avoid death, to deny it, is to deny life itself. They are mutually-arising opposites. One does not exist without the other. If you must deny something, deny the ego-self, because if you can accept death so completely that this self dies away, then you will find the complete fullness of life. And in the nondual reality between life and death, you will discover the secret of immortality.

BEYOND THE VEIL OF DEATH

Many people would like to know what will happen after they die, or what has happened to loved ones who have passed away. It's a fair enough question, but often people want to know so badly they are willing to grasp at and believe any answer that presents itself.

And if they have not realized, totally, what is happening now, in this present moment, how are they to understand death?

Any story that we believe about death, however illuminating, is just a story, another attachment, another delusion. For in the realm of what is, there is no such thing as death. Life and death are only ideas. If you look where you fear the most, you will see. There is nothing hidden from you, except that which you have hidden from yourself.

Consider a rocky coastline, where countless waves come to their end. You cannot stop the waves from crashing on the shore. But nothing is lost. Each wave disintegrates, but the water subsides into the ocean, and the waves come and go without ceasing.

Everything returns to its source.

As you were before birth, that is how you will be in death. And yet … here you are! Unbound by time, life and death, form and formlessness, are united in one indivisible happening. Everything is here and now. Where else could you be? So although there is an end to all things, there is nothing to fear.

The wave has never been other than the ocean. Nor has the ocean ever begrudged the wave.

This present moment you are experiencing is nothing other than the moment in which you were born. It is nothing other than the moment in which you will die. There is no difference. In the ever-changing nature of forms, here and now, there is birth and death in every moment, and yet your true nature is beyond them. Beyond the ego-self, which is the veil of death embodied, you are already beyond life and death, unborn and undying.

The secret of immortality is just a matter of identification. So long as you identify with a sense of self — clinging to memories, thoughts, and emotions, to the illusion of the ego, to past and future, to mind and body — death will be real to you. But when you finally see through these things, freeing your awareness from identification and distinction, death has no hold over you.

It's just Everything

When I say "Everything is here and now," I mean *everything*. This is it, right here, right now, right in front of you. This is everything — everything that is, everything that ever was, and everything that ever will be. All of time and space, every answer ever searched for, it's all right here. There is nothing else but this.

When you realize it, there is nowhere else to look, no place else to be. There is nothing to look forward to, nothing to fear, nothing that can happen at a later time. And there is nothing to regret, no past that can trouble you. There is just this moment now.

If I try now to imagine someplace else, someplace outside of this, where God might be, or where people go when they die, I cannot really do it. I can't imagine anything outside of everything. God is not some distant being in another realm; it is *this* being. This very experience that you are having *is* the divine experience. There is nothing that is not it.

Why don't we see it straight away? It is because we have hidden this divine experience inside our mundane thoughts. By breaking the world up with thoughts, by conceptualizing it, we have conditioned ourselves not to see everything, and we have forgotten how to see nothing. We have lost the ability to see the world undivided.

Perhaps until one is ready, until the ego has run its course, this realization is just too much to bear. It means the end of your self, your life, and the world as you have known it. It means the end of any chances of escape, any hope of future salvation. It means the end of all things. All of that must die away before you can realize the unbound totality of primordial being.

FEAR OF ENLIGHTENMENT

Mention to somebody that who they think they are is only an illusion, and you won't get very far into the conversation before they will either reject the notion outright, based on their own established view of things, or become very uncomfortable. They may become anxious, depressed, or agitated. They may squirm in their seats or abruptly end the conversation.

A person living in a state of delusion will cling to that delusion as if their very life and sanity depended on it. And in a way, from their point of view, it does. Any thought that challenges the validity of the ego-self, any glimpse into a reality beyond it, may be met with extreme unconscious resistance.

Seeing totally through the ego-self means the end of it. You will no longer be able to believe in that entity, or seek any satisfaction through it. A person may sense the infinite being beyond the ego-self — and even long for it — but that very self, formed through attachment, cannot let go. The ego perceives letting go as self-annihilation or insanity and will perpetuate its cycle of attachment as long as possible.

If you catch a momentary glimpse into the enlightened state, as I did on a few occasions throughout my life, you may not recognize it as such. Your ego will step in and tell you it was an anomaly. For a moment, maybe you had a sense of infinite awareness, or a beatific vision, but the ego will say that was just an unusual temporary experience. If anything, the ego will label the experience as a delusion or hallucination. From the ego's point of view, such awareness could not possibly be sustained, nor would it be desirable. It simply cannot conceive how one could live like that, with no sense of self, with no center or boundary, and no desire or attachment.

If you have a deeper or more prolonged experience of this state, with no context or guidance with which to understand it, you may be in for a truly terrifying experience. You may think you are dying or completely losing your mind. I had just such an experience during my college years.

I was walking home from class, and as I passed through a crowd of students, I saw an empty can of Coke on the pavement. My gaze stayed on it just a moment too long, and it was like a switch went off inside me. Instantly, the whole world changed. I stared up the street and the view seemed flat and strange. And as I walked, everything grew even stranger. I felt like the world had become unhinged, and I started to get scared. What was happening? I ran back to my apartment, up the stairs, inside, locked the door, and lay down on the floor, trying to catch my breath. For hours I stayed there, staring up at the ceiling. I thought I was really going insane. I didn't know who I was anymore. I thought I might end up in an institution and I wouldn't even know it. I saw the end of myself, and it scared the hell out of me. Bit by bit, after four or five hours, I started to feel like myself again, and the fear that gripped me subsided. I went on with my life, with no idea that I had perhaps seen into the very truth I sought.

This fear of enlightenment may manifest in many ways, from the most dramatic to the most subtle and mundane, depending on your thoughts and your state of awareness. You may long for awakening, but at the same time experience a deeply-rooted resistance to it, sensing it requires the end of your self.

If you experience this fear in any form, try not to resist it, deny it, or struggle with it. Instead, look directly at your fear, and thus see with clarity that it is simply a sensation arising within consciousness. There is truly nothing to be afraid of. The end of the self seems very real while you are in the grips of delusion, but beyond it one realizes there was never really any self to die away.

Saying Goodbye

At some point you will have to let go of everything. There is nothing that will not pass away — no thought, no experience, no idea, no system, no object, no self, no person. All will return to the formless primordial ocean of consciousness. In the very next moment or at the hour of your death, you will have to relinquish it all.

In the weeks that immediately followed my awakening, I sometimes wondered what had happened to me? Where had my life gone? As strange as it seems, I wondered, where had all my problems gone? Sure, they were problems, but they were *my* problems. Where had I gone? I could no longer find any sense of myself.

One evening, I lay in bed reading the final chapters in Joel Morwood's book, *The Way of Selflessness*. I had skipped to the end, and was trying to understand what had really happened to me. There, I came across these lines from Rumi:

> Footprints come to the Ocean's shore.
> Therein, no trace remains.

Upon reading these words, I was overwhelmed with grief and joy. Sitting in bed that night, I mourned my own death, for somehow in that moment, it really sank in that I was gone — really gone. That person that I had been for all those years, and everything about him that made him seem real, had really vanished. He had been nothing more than footsteps leading to this ocean's shore.

I wept as one weeps at the passing of a loved one, mourning the loss of their qualities, both good and bad, at their familiar presence, at their endearing and troublesome quirks, at their particular tangle of thoughts and concerns. But simultaneously, I wept with joy at the beauty of it all, in the bliss of that ocean to which we return. For when you give it all up, relinquishing everything, something wonderful happens. And therein, no trace remains.

PART III

TEACHINGS

There is no word
For the way
Wildflowers sway
In the spring breeze.

Can you see it?
Can you feel it?

Beyond the flowers,
Beyond the breeze,
I am that,
I am that,
I am that.

Systems of Thought

Religions, philosophies, myths, traditions, sciences, and spiritual teachings are all different ways of creating systems of thoughts, concepts, and things. The absolute truth, however, cannot be a thought, concept, or thing. In a manner of speaking, it is nothing, and this is why no system of thought can touch it. However, this *nothing* is really the source of everything. So when you let go of things and systems of things, and really see it, you will see it in all things. And I dare say you will be filled with a joy you never imagined possible.

From the point of view of somebody who sees the world through any system of thought, this may sound like nonsense or like the truth itself. But either way, that person is not seeing the total picture, and they will try to incorporate or reject any new thought according to their current thought system. And all systems are, in some sense, hermetic traps, assuring their adherents rarely see beyond them. The trouble with religious systems is they go too far into belief. The trouble with scientific systems is they don't go far enough into doubt. The trouble with philosophical systems is they get lost in a labyrinth of thoughts, words, and distinctions. Finally, various spiritual systems may employ all these traps, as well as the very clever traps that proclaim the way beyond all traps.

This is why I must be adamant in restating that this book is not meant to support or refute any system of thought, whether it be religious, scientific, philosophical, or spiritual. Those are different discussions entirely. For our purpose here, all systems of thought are a distraction. They are forms, which when clung to, prevent the realization of the formless.

It's very simple. If we cling to thoughts, if we cling to things and believe in them, they will shape our reality, and that's all we will ever see. We will never see beyond them. Should we catch a glimpse of nothing, we will pass right over it as we sit admiring the precious things we cling to, or as we reach for the next thought or the next thing to grab hold of.

It's not that we must cease all thinking. We cannot do that, any more than we can stop all water from flowing or stop all the stars from burning. It's not that we must abolish all things, or systems of things. But we must see that they are only functions of thought, and then see through thought to the emptiness within.

Empty yourself completely. Discard all your treasured beliefs. Let go of the person you thought you were or wanted to be. Wipe away all memories of an ancient past. Discard all predictions of an uncertain future. Beneath your left heel stomp out fear, and beneath your right heel crush all hope. Become nobody … become nothing … and you will see: it is from this nothing that all things have their origin.

The Roots of Evil

Some people become hung up on the problem of evil. If everything is divine, then what could justify the tremendous suffering and evil in the world? Why would anyone say such a situation was acceptable, let alone perfect?

Of course, the problem of evil is a question many people have wrestled with. My own answer is not complicated. It's basically what Buddhists have been saying for a long time. Suffering is a result of delusion. It's just that we usually think about this in terms of our own suffering, and not the whole big problem of suffering and evil in general. But the big problem is not different from the small problem.

To say suffering is acceptable is not quite right, but good and evil arise mutually, and it is clear that everything is happening according to the way things happen. In that sense everything is perfect. An evil man is not evil because he is thinking clearly. He is evil precisely because he is deluded. And to the extent of his delusions and his desires, he will suffer and cause suffering. To remove delusion is to relieve suffering, on whatever level. In the absence of delusion, joy is present and compassion flourishes.

Jesus was not kidding around when he said to love your enemies, or when he said "Father, forgive them, for they know not what they do." But he wasn't saying murder was acceptable, or that we should condone evil acts. Horrific acts go hand in hand with extreme delusion and extreme suffering. But instead of hating evil-doers, why not see what's really happening? What is the source of this thing we call evil? How does it grow and spread?

Fighting to relieve suffering is commendable, but as long as there is someone who desires to do good, there will be evil. As long as we remain deluded, embracing our desires and self-centered worldview, we are a part of that problem. As long as we are in conflict with ourselves, we will continue to do horrible things to each other. We're all wrapped up in it. There is no way out, except to wake up to a reality beyond delusion.

Why Delusion

To say suffering is a result of delusion might seem like putting off the problem. If suffering is a result of delusion, then why delusion? This is another difficult question, and the closer we get to the origin of things, the more difficult it is to answer intelligibly. The question *Why is there delusion?* is somewhat like asking why is there something rather than nothing. I propose no metaphysical solutions, but for the sake of discussion let's throw out a couple ideas and see where they take us.

Nobody is really running the universe in the way that is suggested by the question. There is no big boss somewhere setting up the game and calling all the shots. If there *is* anyone running the universe like this, consider that you may be it. For without separation, we are the whole process of what's going on, and that process, if we can call it that, guides everything that is, including suffering. It is only the illusion of separation that keeps us from waking up to our role in it all.

Who decides there is a lot of suffering in the world? Who says it's too much? How would anyone know what is a lot? There could be ten times as much, a hundred times even. Who is it who suffers? Who wants to do something about it? These are the questions we must inquire into.

In Hinduism, there is an idea of God as a kind of actor, hiding within each being, playing all the parts in a kind of divine play. Of course, God is such a good actor that he hides even from his own true nature. He completely fools himself, and this self-delusion keeps the whole drama of the world going. There is something to this, but it may not be satisfying if you don't see it and are deeply troubled by suffering. So let's try a different train of thought, and a different narrative.

Delusion is a rather negative word. Nobody wants to think they are deluded, so this very idea can be a stumbling block that reinforces the ego. But the Sanskrit word *maya,* so often translated as "illusion," can also mean "magic" or "power." Looking at the world historically, the illusion of a separate self may have granted some benefit, socially, linguistically, or cognitively. Perhaps this illusion came with the ability to remember the past, plan for the future, and coordinate novel group and individual actions. Seen this way, the magic and power of maya becomes more clear.

In this story, delusion may be a facilitative or functional illusion. But we can't have the good without the bad. If we take all the benefits such magic grants us, we must also contend with the evil such power breeds, and all the terrible suffering created by selfish desires and misguided delusions. That is the path human beings have ventured down. But from the beginning, there has always been a way out, an awakening to our true, unseparated consciousness. There's something to this explanation too, but let's try one last idea, with a twist.

There is something strange going on here. There can be no awakening without delusion, just as there can be no life without death. Like something and nothing, delusion and enlightenment arise mutually. It is the very suffering caused by delusion that draws one toward awakening. Only through this separation from our true nature can we be reunited with it. This idea brings us full circle in a way, back to the divine drama, for it is being itself that manifests, separating itself from itself, creating the very delusions which will draw it back into itself. And that being is you. Your true nature is beyond delusion *and* awakening.

The ocean of delusion that seems to exist between you and enlightenment is itself an illusion. Reach the far shore and you will realize no distance has been crossed. These are all just thoughts. They are images, and as images they are illusions themselves. So even if they work for you, don't become attached to them. Tell me instead, in this very moment, before you can think another thought, what delusions *are* there?

The Problem with Problems

Many seemingly difficult problems, such as the problems of why evil exists, of free will, of how consciousness arises, of why there is something rather than nothing, of what happens after death, and so many others that have perplexed and troubled people's minds throughout the ages are really only problems from particular points of view.

Such questions arise in relation to various systems of thought that we cling to. Relative to a system of thought, they may or may not be solvable, but the problems themselves are a product of clinging to conceptual frameworks. This is very difficult to see until you see it totally, until you awake to a reality beyond all systems of thought.

Evil is a concept. Consciousness is an idea. Something and nothing imply each other. And death is only a problem when you assume there is such a thing and that you are not dead already. Clinging to ideas automatically attaches us to all the problems that arise in relation to those concepts or systems of thought.

In essence, the real answer cannot be explained. Everything we can say is false on some level, because the whole truth, the totality of it, cannot be bound by any conceptual framework. It is the reality upon which conceptual frameworks can arise, not the other way around. And such problems can only manifest in relation to those conceptual frameworks, not in relation to reality itself, which is beyond all things.

This is the problem with problems, both the personal problem as well as the grand philosophical problem. We're creating them all. All problems are self-created. There are no exceptions.

The Importance of Waking Up

Is waking up important? Only you can answer that question. Whatever I may say will make no difference whatsoever to you, and is beside the point. If you think it's important, then it is; if you don't, then it isn't. But this much I can say: when you've had enough, when you're tired of pain and suffering, when you're frustrated beyond all reason, when you can't stand yourself or the world any longer, complete liberation is possible.

The recognition of pure consciousness is the only real solution to the problems of your mind, as well as the problems of the world. Ultimately, there is no difference between these sets of problems. World problems are caused by, are a reflection of, and ultimately simply are, nothing but mind problems. You cannot completely solve such a problem if you cannot see through it clearly, and seeing through it clearly, there is no problem to solve.

To see through the illusions of the ego and the world, and to wake up in this life is to finally see clearly. It is to simply see what's really happening. With all delusions unveiled, you will realize this very world as the divine world, and recognize your true self as the divine Self. Bliss and beauty radiates through everything. Love and compassion take their natural course. Eternity is found in this very moment.

Some speculate that awakening is a movement in the evolution of human consciousness, others that it is the last chance to save humanity from destroying itself. But these are only speculations, only ideas, and in any case we would just have to wait and find out. So in the meantime, is it important for you to realize the truth? Is it important to know God? Is it important to forgive, to let go of fear, to be at peace? It may sound as if these are leading questions, but truly, only you can answer them.

There's nothing wrong with saying no, that you're enjoying your life as it is. It can be said that wherever you happen to be, whatever you happen to be doing or thinking *is* what's happening, and it is the beauty and the vast intelligence of being in action. However, many people who would read a book like this already think waking up is important and, more significantly, may have already taken steps toward awakening, so that has been the focus here throughout.

In my own case, I had given up thinking anything like this was possible, let alone important. I had given up on everything, and then realization dawned. Now I can say, for those who genuinely seek it, no price is too high to realize the truth. So if you decide this is important to you, what will you do? Only you can say.

THERE IS NO METHOD

If you decide it's important to wake up, or if you read this book and think you would like to experience awakening or attain enlightenment, you are likely to find yourself with a whole new set of problems. Namely, how? And as we will see, it is a rather tricky set of problems.

I want to be absolutely clear about this from the start. Although I will suggest various practices, strictly speaking there is no method for this realization. Some things do seem to make it more likely, but there are no techniques you can master that will get you there. There is nothing you can do or not do that will simply make it come about.

Why? There are a number of reasons, some of which you may already be struggling with. One is that you imagine your objective is somehow far away, that the way is somehow obstructed, that the journey is difficult, and the end lies somewhere in the future. But it's right in front of you. It *is* you. How can there be a method? It's right here now! But you have hidden this truth from yourself. Only you know exactly how you have hidden it, and with what you have covered it up ... but you have hidden that from yourself as well.

Furthermore, you imagine that *you* will experience enlightenment, that the sense of self will gain something, becoming wiser and more complete in some way. But the experience is a selfless experience — that is, without any sense of individual self. Once you have seen through the illusion of self, through and through, there *is* no self to become enlightened. So there is nothing to gain. It is already here ... it's *you* who are not.

So how does realization happen? Certainly, it is not a matter of ordinary knowledge or understanding, nor of doing something or not doing something. You need not be a saint or a monk. You need not study texts or master skills. You need not have a teacher or meditate for hours on end. You need not journey to another country, or follow any religion. Unless, of course, you think that's what you need. For if you really think you need something, you might have to do it before you're able to let go.

Ultimately, all paths are ways of delaying realization. Frequently, however, one must go all the way to the end of a path to find that out. If one is relentless in their pursuit of the truth, all such paths will self-destruct in the end. All methods fail. Then, perhaps, one will be ready to wake up.

It Cannot be Attained

The enlightenment that is sought after can never be attained. When we think of awakening, we may think we can't imagine what it would be like, but nevertheless we imagine something, however vague. And we may think the ego-self is only an illusion, but nevertheless we seek attainment for it. We should be honest about this and not dismiss it.

There is no self to be enlightened though, just as there is no self to be deluded. The ego-self and all separation *is* delusion. Your true nature is already the enlightenment you seek. That is the divine Self realized in awakening. It need not attain anything, for there is no lack within it. It need not seek, for it is present already.

There is nothing to find, for that which you seek is not a thing. Whenever you imagine that there is something out there to be attained, something that you feel you don't have, something that you have not yet realized, you simply reinforce the illusion of the ego, and the delusion of self and other.

That which is happening before you now is all there is. You already are it! The mental and the biological, the positive and the negative, the past and the future, the inside and the outside, are all within you. All that's left is to recognize it.

You Cannot Transform Yourself

Let's say you have it in mind to improve yourself psychologically in some way. Maybe you wish to be more loving and compassionate, or less anxious and afraid. And to accomplish this, you set about trying to change yourself in various ways. But there is a fundamental problem. That is, the person you wish to change, and the person responsible for the change, are one and the same person.

The fact of the matter is that you *are* anxious and afraid, and no amount of effort or force of will can change this. It is like trying to command yourself to go to sleep, or like trying to force your body to relax. You cannot do it, because the you who you identify with is the source of the problem.

When you first hear this, you will likely think it's not right. There must be some way around this. Surely, with practice, you can teach yourself to relax. Surely you can train yourself to have more compassion. It may be difficult. It may take a long time. But surely you can do it!

Ask yourself though, seriously, who is it that will institute these changes? Who and what, exactly, are you? Are you the anxious you, the you who says you must stop being so anxious, or are you something beyond both of these, or beyond that? If you can change your anxiety, then you must somehow not be limited by it. And if you are already not limited by it, what change is needed?

Your anxiety is produced by your desire to change yourself, by your very feeling that there is something wrong that must be changed. Your fear is a function of your desire to hold on to the self you wish to change. You are creating your problems. You do not need to do anything to change yourself, even if you could. You need only to stop creating more problems.

Don't get me wrong, real transformation is possible, transformation beyond your wildest dreams. But you cannot remove a problem with a problem. It's like trying to clear muddy water by sweeping it with your hand. The more you sweep, the more cloudy the water becomes.

What then can be done? Simply this: see that you are not the things you wish to change. Don't try to change anything, but whatever comes up, whatever thoughts or feelings, just look at them, be present with them. Identify thoughts as thoughts, feelings as feelings, sensations as sensations. Thus you will stop identifying yourself with those thoughts, feelings, and sensations.

You may find yourself not wanting to do this, because you feel somehow you're nothing without these things. That is just a feeling. You may think this will never work because you're not really doing anything. That is just a thought. You may have the sensation of being overwhelmed or of falling. That is just a sensation. Pay these things no mind. Just persist in this. Transformation will take care of itself.

GATELESS GATEWAYS

Everything is a gateway to awakening. Pain, grief, frustration, boredom, and suffering can be highly-effective teachers. And without delusion, there would be no self or world illusion to awaken from. So wherever you are, whatever is before you now, that is the entrance.

See the totality of what is actually happening. Observe any sensations and sense perceptions in your awareness. See the thoughts and emotions that form and the course they take. What else is there? Inquire into the nature of these things, and into the nature of the self, the world, time, and death.

The passages in this book are not written in order to explain any concept or create any system of thought or belief, but to act as gateways. That is their ultimate purpose.

Remember: there is no wrong thought, and there is no real path. All thoughts are only thoughts. All paths are illusory. You cannot make a mistake. You cannot break reality or cause it to falter. Ultimately, you cannot prevent your awakening any more than you can cause it.

It may seem as if there is a barrier to enlightenment. But if you see anything totally, be it the self, time, thought, or just an ordinary object, the whole house of cards may collapse around you. Once you have passed through the imagined barrier, there is no barrier. You will realize not only that you are everything that is unfolding now, but that you always have been, and always will be.

Leave Everything as It Is

Total transformation of consciousness cannot come about by changing things or doing things. Of course, you cannot stop doing things altogether. But there's no point in trying to transform yourself by making a bunch of changes to your life circumstances. The circumstances have nothing to do with it. And there's no point in trying to change the world. Just stop trying to change things all together.

We are constantly struggling against ourselves and the world. We are always trying to improve our situation, improve ourselves, change the world, build a better society, get rid of bad habits, be happier, improve our relationships, find new relationships, lose weight, make ourselves smarter, healthier, more compassionate, more spiritual, or whatever the case may be. But we will never be satisfied that way.

This constant striving is actually the source of our dissatisfaction and the reason we feel we must improve something. We don't know it, but we're caught in a feedback loop of epic proportions. The more we want things to change, the more we resist what is, the more frustrated we become. Look, things will change — trust me. We don't need rush ahead or try to force things. Any attempt to do so is illusory and can only cause more frustration.

In one form after another, you have set yourself the task of solving unsolvable problems. Let's say you want to be happy. By wanting to be happy, you define yourself as being unhappy. How then are you to be happy now? If you can't be happy now, then when? Let's say you'd like to work out all your issues, all your blocks and hang-ups. This is always something that must happen over time, coming to resolution in some imagined future. But the future will never arrive. There is only now. If you put it off, you put it off forever.

Likewise, you will never arrange the circumstances of your life or the world in such a way that everything is good, any more than you can arrange an object such that it has an upside but no downside. The good and the bad arise mutually. The greater the improvements you imagine and desire, the more wrong you will see with the world. If you think you can somehow get to the end of the list and get everything arranged just so, you are mistaken.

Everything is constantly falling apart. There is no way to stop it. There is no ground to stand on. There is nothing to hold on to. Everything is changing already. What can anybody do but go with it?

Strive with All Your Might

If you feel you absolutely must change things, if you feel you must work to achieve enlightenment, or suffer to deserve it, by all means do it. Strive with all your might. Create a struggle of monumental proportions if that's what seems necessary. But when you've had enough, remember you can let it go. You can leave everything as it is at any time.

I say strive with all your might not because you will ever achieve lasting satisfaction with such a struggle, but because eventually you may come to see the futility of it as a means to satisfaction. After all, you are only struggling with yourself. In the realm of what is, all conflicts, all struggles, are an illusion.

So if you can't escape the feeling that you need to pursue this thing, then don't hold back. If you persist long enough, with sufficient effort, you may realize it — not when you win the struggle, but when you finally give up on winning, when you finally see through the illusion of struggle all together.

This is the hidden goal behind virtually all spiritual practices — be it meditation, inquiry, prayer, or devotion — just to get to a point where you basically give up. I struggled mightily for many years, and then it ended. I didn't win or lose, or even resolve the struggle in any way. I finally saw that my whole struggle was pointless and I gave up. Then all struggle ended.

So if you are following a path like this, and you're determined not to give up, then follow it for as long as it takes … all the way to the end. Don't become complacent and settle in along the way. Don't give up. Follow it until the whole thing unravels in front of you, until your whole world is falling apart around you. Then at last you can dive in and go with it. Eventually you'll realize you have nothing to lose.

It's So Tricky

If you try to figure all this stuff out and settle it once and for all in your mind, you will outwit yourself at every turn. That's because it's not a matter of intellectually understanding some set of logical arguments. Nor is it a matter of believing in some postulated set of concepts. Therefore, it will always slip away from your grasp. You have to really see it, but for you to make this happen is a special type of conundrum. It is, in fact, the impossible problem itself.

If I suggest you stop desiring, you will find yourself desiring not to desire. If I say you should have no expectation, you will work to banish every expectation from your mind, expecting something to happen when you do. If I recommend you let go of everything, you will hang on to that very idea. If I insist you get rid of the ego, you will make an ego trip out of it. If I say you must be absolutely free, you will bind yourself to this imperative.

You see the problem. Again and again you will encounter some version of this problem when you try to figure this out. So if you *are* trying to figure it out, this is the actual problem you have to wrestle with. What is the central issue? Why is it so difficult? It's like trying to look directly at the back of your own head. It's not behind you, and it's not in front of you. In Zen they say such problems are like swallowing a ball of hot iron. You can't get it down, and you can't cough it back up.

The difficulty is simply this: you're in your own way. You might ask "How do I do get out of my way?" To which I would say "Not like that." That's just another impossible problem. You might then ask "Okay, *why* am I in my own way?" To which I would say "Which one of you is asking?"

You see, there really is no *you*. Or, stated another way, you are the totality of what is going on. There is no difficulty. Everything is perfectly clear.

Voluntary and Involuntary

Consider the way we tend to divide the world into what is voluntary and what is involuntary — what you do and what happens to you — and you may begin to chip away at the illusion of the self. Ask yourself: Who is it who does these things, and to whom are these things happening? What are the limits of doing and happening?

I think, I decide, I move. These are all generally categorized as voluntary acts. On the other hand, *I grow old, I fall asleep, I wake up* are not considered voluntary. They just happen. It's like saying "I circulate my blood" or "I regulate my endocrine system." These are more happenings than doings. We do not will them to happen, nor need we understand how the body is doing them. But are such happenings really so different than thinking and moving?

Can you predict what your next thought will be? What your next memory will be? When you decide to open your hand or close your hand, how do you decide? Do you decide to decide, or do you just do it? In the present moment, without the involvement of time, memory, or recursive thoughts, it all just happens. A decision happens. The hand opens. It is only because, through conditioning, we identify with certain processes, such as thinking, deciding, and moving, that they seem voluntary to us. We have created our identity out of those things, so naturally we take credit for them.

Have you noticed that when things go well for people, when they are successful, they tend to take credit for it? They are successful because they're hard working, smart, tough, and disciplined. But when things don't go well, even for the very same people, they often claim outside circumstances are responsible. This very natural tendency is simply a way of bolstering the ego, of solidifying and protecting one's identity. It happens simply by shifting this boundary between what you do and what happens to you. In fact, it could be said that this *is* the boundary of the ego.

This identification process and the manipulation of ego boundaries can only take place in time. We have a thought, for example, and then take credit for it. We think, *That was my thought.* Something happens, and then through memory and reflection, we take credit or assign responsibility. To create an identity we must shift backward and forward in time. But if we examine ourselves absolutely in this present moment, it's quite clear we're nobody, and all of this — everything, inside and outside — is all just a wonderful happening.

If you can really see there is no difference between things we attribute to doing and things we attribute to happening, and the boundary of the ego disappears, you may also have the feeling that everything is your doing. When you cease to identify with the time-bound ego, you are confronted with the present moment — this singular grand unfolding process — and since you are still aware, what else could you be but that? You are the sun shining and the trees growing. You are the clouds moving and the rain falling. You're doing it all. You don't know how you're doing it, but you're doing it.

In truth, there is no voluntary or involuntary, no doing or happening, no you or not-you. There is no word for this. Some call it Tao, others God, others void. This can be useful or misleading, but ultimately there really is no word for it. All words discriminate, and this is all encompassing, complete, and without discrimination. Thus is it said: the Tao that can be named is not the eternal Tao.

You Are What Is

So whatever reality is, it is not fundamentally divided into individual things and discrete events, which are distinctions made in thought and language, but not in reality. The division into things and events is the product of thought, which is itself a kind of thing or event. Perhaps the first thing thought separates from the rest of reality is the self. And through conditioning, everything else follows, including time, space, and all the objects and events contained within them. And so we come to feel the self is what we are, and reality is somehow separate from us.

Finding ourselves in this strange predicament, it is no wonder that we feel alienated, confused, trapped, and unsatisfied. But it is possible, first, to recognize through thought that you are not separate from reality, and secondly to realize beyond thought the reality that you are — to know and experience that you are what is.

Let's consider the universe as it's generally thought about and described today. The present universe with all its billions of galaxies appears to have started from a kind of explosion that flung out all matter, time and space, and everything that's in it. From that, galaxies took shape, stars ignited, planets formed, life began, organisms grew, people evolved, and finally you were born, grew up, and began having these thoughts now. It is all one ongoing process. So leaving aside the arbitrary, thought-created divisions between events and things, you simply *are* this process as a whole.

Maybe this makes sense as an argument, but you just don't feel like you are the universe. That's all right. The feeling that you are not the whole universe is another part of the process. And in any case, the point here is just to explain a certain way of looking at things, to see how it doesn't make sense to separate yourself out from the rest of reality. Whatever is happening, you are a part of it, and left un-parted, undivided, you are the whole of it. What else could you be?

Look at the objects around you. What really separates you from any of those things? The atoms of your skin are continuous with the atoms of the surrounding environment, and there is more space in those atoms than anything else. The atoms themselves are made of things whose status as things at all becomes increasingly more dubious as you go down in scale.

But regardless of how you conceptualize objects, your sense of self is in the mind, and everything you see and hear and touch are also experienced in the mind. And you are creating the division between them — between subject and object — in the mind. Without this division, without this bubble of the self, there is no separation between you and everything that is, was, or ever will be.

We cling to various things and events in a misguided and desperate attempt to reintegrate ourselves into reality. In this way, our desire and our clinging are symptoms of our separation, and our longing to remember our true nature, our fundamental being, our bliss, at one with all that is. But you cannot return by grasping, for grasping itself creates the illusion of separation. You cannot go back. There is no back. You cannot go forward. There is no forward. But it is always present. Beyond words, beyond thought, you are what is.

Chances of Awakening

How many enlightened people are there in the world, and what are the chances of actual realization? I don't know the answers to these questions. It seems relatively rare, but for anyone already in the midst of their journey, it could be imminent. There's no way to know. All I can do is try to convey what happened to me, and speculate as to what might increase the chances of awakening.

In one sense, your true nature is ultimately unavoidable, so awakening is inevitable. However, it is not inevitable for *you* — that is, for your ego-self. The ego can never awaken. The state of enlightenment cannot be grasped or held by the mind. But if one sees clearly and totally through the mind, then awakening is assured, for it is always there, waiting for us, without exception.

Many people, I think, have experienced glimpses, but without final and complete realization. This was certainly the case in my life before awakening. Such glimpses are significant, important clues, but they are not enlightenment. They are markers along the path, blessings in their own right, but they are not the end.

In my own case, a number of circumstances led me on to the end. But whether the circumstances or the path came first is impossible to say. And because the situations of each person's life are different, one cannot depend entirely on an established route. One must, on some level, find their own way, even if practicing within an existing tradition. Nevertheless, an examination of my circumstances may offer some insight.

My family moved a number of times during some very formative years — around the ages of five, ten, and sixteen. As a result, I made several major readjustments, and along the way I became very comfortable spending time alone. These readjustments may have interrupted some conditioning that otherwise would have gone deeper. And eventually, through solitude I began to explore meditation and inquiry.

I traveled widely in my late teens and twenties, and was exposed to a broad spectrum of cultures and people. I was deeply affected by the suffering I saw, and was overwhelmed by the sheer multitude and variety of possible lives. Some of these experiences shook me to the core. They uncovered a raw and unexplored region of my heart that I could never again completely cover up.

I became interested in spiritual wisdom, science, and philosophy at a fairly young age. After a relaxed Christian upbringing, in college I gravitated toward interests in Hinduism and Buddhism, as well as physics, philosophy, and literary theory. Later in life, I developed an actual interest in Christianity, even becoming a practicing Catholic for a number of years.

I dedicated myself to a regular practice of martial arts for some twenty-five years. My primary study for a long time was Aikido, an art rooted in the spiritual ideas of its founder. Later, I began training in Systema, another art with spiritual underpinnings, and whose very training methods aimed at understanding all aspects of oneself.

I fell deeply in love several times in my life, but these relationships dissolved in tumultuous or mundane circumstances, or else crumbled beneath the impossible weight of my own romantic ideas and selfish desires.

Finally, I set myself the task of somehow becoming a successful writer. It was a goal that demanded sacrifices and I made them. For many years I worked at writing with dogged determination, and with very little by way of recognition, encouragement, or financial reward.

The experience of these circumstances was not always a pretty picture. I was a stubborn person with high ideals, lofty ideas, strong passions, and with great longing and ambition. And in everything, I was looking for a satisfaction I could not find. I frequently felt out of step with the world around me. And while my path included some soaring heights of love, adventure, and accomplishment, it was also a path of solitude, sorrow, heartbreak, disillusionment, pain, and failure.

When I consider all this, one thing becomes clear. There is a kind of thread that runs through all the various twists and turns.

I was on quest to understand myself, to figure out the mysteries of life and the world, to acquire mastery over them, to express my deepest thoughts and feelings, to attain true love, truth, and exaltation … which is perhaps to say, redemption, salvation, and liberation.

All that seeking had to come to an end, had to run its course before realization. And yet, even my unorthodox path suggests the chances of awakening may depend on engaging in a spiritual quest, in dedicating oneself to some practice and teachings, of surrendering the self, and of relentlessly searching for the truth in whatever comes your way. You may face many twists and turns, and great difficulties upon this quest, but the fruits of its reward reveal the blessings of an infinite grace.

There must be an end to all things, but how we get there is a mystery every person must unravel for themselves. Anything that reveals the illusion of the self and the delusions of the ego, or draws attention to the desires and attachments that keep us bound to suffering, could increase the chances of awakening.

However you proceed, I can assure you that the way passes through where you're at.

GRADUAL OR SUDDEN AWAKENING

There seems to be some debate about whether awakening is a gradual process or a sudden event. Of course, it should be said right away that this debate is about concepts of awakening and not awakening itself. It is a conceptual argument. So there is no absolutely true answer. That being said, a few things could be explored on either side of the debate.

Awakening is the culmination of everything that has happened in your life. There is not a single thing that is not a part of this process. So in this way it could be viewed as gradual. It begins the moment you make the first distinction between self and other, and ends the moment you see through it all.

There is no way to know for sure where someone is in this process, since there are no steps, no levels, no signs, no gradations — no path. The process itself is a maze of confusion. It is itself the Gordian knot of delusion that must at last be severed.

When the sword of truth finally cuts through that knot, however, it must happen instantaneously. Why? Because time itself is part of the delusion, and the awakened state is a timeless state. When you finally see through all delusion, there is no past or future anymore. So there is no room for gradual progress, or any progress at all for that matter. There is only now. And for this reason, awakening must be sudden.

Ultimately, awakening can never happen in the future, which is only imaginary. All such notions are simply putting it off. It can only happen now.

Everything Runs its Course

Water makes no effort to find its way. A river does not exert itself to flow into the ocean. If the water hits an obstacle, it may pool up and eddy for a while before moving on, but it does not dismay. It all gets where it's going by not doing anything. And like this, everything runs its course.

The seasons do not rush to arrive. Nor do they hurry to depart.

All striving, all effort, is illusory. When we struggle, we create a problem and struggle with it. When we fight, we create an enemy and fight with it. And even so, though we may not realize it, there are still no obstructions. All our striving is not the way, but it is not separate from the way.

In truth, there is no need to force anything. Nor is there any need to choose one direction over another. Such things are only a function of your imagination. What's happening is already happening. You cannot stop it. You cannot deviate from it. You cannot change its course, for no matter how hard you try, you cannot *not do* what you are doing in the present moment.

For the most part, people don't see this because they are identified with the ego, and therefore bound in time. Through memory and anticipation, hopes and fears, the ego appears to be an agent of change, but it is like a face seen in the clouds. It is like a name given to the nameless. The unnamed is already unfolding harmoniously. All that's left is for you to recognize that you are not apart from it. You *are* it.

So whatever you do, do it without doing. Have patience. But don't have patience in the sense that you endure the present while waiting for the future. There is no such future. Have patience in the sense that you are present in this moment, and in accord with what is actually happening.

Everything runs its course. You are no different.

Dark Night

You may come to a place when all the things that gave a sense of meaning to your life no longer do. You no longer believe in whatever you had believed in. All conceptual understanding, all philosophies, all models of reality seem vacuous. All systems of thought appear, at last, inadequate, and you are left with the raw experiences of a seemingly meaningless life, day after day, year after year until you die. It all feels hollow, worthless. And no matter how you try to conjure some meaning back into it, to restoke the fire of belief once more, it proves futile.

This could be brought on by the failure of a relentless inquiry, the collapse of some belief system, or a sudden unexpected loss of something which gave great meaning to your life. The loss of a loved one, for example, a catastrophic injury, failing health, or financial ruin. And while this dark night can manifest as a kind of depression, it is really a spiritual, existential crisis. All conceptual frameworks for making sense of life and all internal stories for making sense of the self have ceased to be meaningful. But you have not yet let go, so the fruits of transformed consciousness cannot be experienced. Instead you are filled with a kind of dread, which you must cope with, one way or another.

For me, although I had struggled with bouts of depression since my early twenties, this dark night really started with the breakup of my marriage, around which I had framed a story of deep romantic attachment, spiritual meaning, and absolute commitment. When that framework of meaning collapsed, I began to reevaluate my whole life. It created a kind of chain reaction, and one by one, over the course of about ten years, all the stories I had formed to give my life meaning began to unravel, along with any new stories I tried to form. They all self-destructed until I found myself one night saying to my girlfriend, "I'm done."

"What do you mean, you're done?" she said. "You're done with what?"

"The whole thing," I said. "I'm finished. I'm out of the game. I have no opinions anymore. I have nothing to say about anything."

That was maybe a few months before awakening entirely transformed my life.

So if you find yourself in a place where life seems to lose all its meaning, know that it is only the imagined meaning that is passing away. It's only the stories you have told to yourself about what life means that are ending. And while losing your belief in them can feel catastrophic, overwhelming, unbearable, enraging ... there is a light beyond that present darkness. You transcend all imagined meanings, all personal narratives. Your life has a meaning beyond all that, but it is a meaning that cannot be conceptualized, explained, or turned into a personal narrative. It is a meaning beyond you, beyond your self.

From that dark place, maybe some people rebuild a new conceptual and narrative framework. Maybe that's possible. But it is far better to leave that all behind, and awaken to the presence of what is truly happening, diving into the eternal now. For this to happen, all remnants of meaning, all fragments of conceptual belief, must be burned away. Move toward emptiness, letting go of any remaining attachments. Accept that there is nothing to gain any longer. There is nobody to become. The dark night is a kind of purgatory, in the interstices between life, death, transformation, and rebirth. Already there is nothing that is not God, but here at last we recognize it through and through. The final separation dissolves, and the truth is realized. You and everything you perceive are already one with God.

COMPLETE REALIZATION

What is really involved in complete realization? Although I've said a lot already, and recognizing that all attempts to be accurate here must fail, let's examine the question. For in the moment of my own awakening, something absolutely incredible happened which I still cannot account for. And this shift in perception, this change in consciousness, at once subtle and cataclysmic, sudden and permanent, is at the heart of what I am trying to convey.

Something takes place that is not one's doing, that is not of a person's mind or body, something that changes everything. And that everlasting instant, in which it seems the whole universe turns inside out, like consciousness imploding and exploding simultaneously — only without violence — that movement, that something, really is just indescribable. It instantly cuts through the veil of illusion that we have hitherto called the self and the world, time and death, and all the dualities of things and of thought. It cracks the delusion of a person's mind as if it were an egg, and from it one's true being wakes up and recognizes itself.

So this change — its realization and the awareness it reveals — lies beyond time and all explanation, beyond thought and words. But let's say a little more to see if we can tease out some way of understanding what it entails.

Seeing through the illusion of the ego and the complete emptying of the self is only part of it. When identification with the ego ceases, there is suddenly no seer or thinker or doer. There is consciousness, but because there is no identification with the ego, the self cannot be located, and there is no inside or outside anymore. Without a subject, subject-object duality collapses, and there is no longer any separation between you and what you perceive.

And still, that is only part of it. One also realizes that just as the self is an empty illusion, so is everything else! The body, the mind, the trees, time and space, the moon and stars, the whole universe and everything in it are as illusory as the ego. There is consciousness itself — whatever that is — but without any subject or objects. All things perceived are but empty forms arising in this one being. And with this complete realization, our eyes open to reality, to the divine eternal happening.

It is not just subject-object duality that collapses, but all dualities all together. That is why it is so ineffable, so without definable qualities or attributes, so inexplicable, and so mysterious to those who are hypnotized by the delusions of dualistic viewpoints. For it is this nondual awareness that lies beyond words and beyond thought. That is what one might call enlightenment, God, or simply the Truth.

But none of this unfolds bit by bit the way it sounds, nor with any sort of chronology or intellectual understanding. To break it down in any way is misleading. Total perception happens all at once. The whole house of cards collapses, and realization dawns with sudden completeness, full of mysterious joy, radiant with bliss. It's only later that one can try to make some sense of it, communicate it, or write about it. But all such attempts are in the dualistic terms of language. So nothing I've said here even really comes close. It is truly beyond words. You will just have to see for yourself.

Short Answers
about Enlightenment

Q: Do you really consider yourself enlightened?

A: The short answer is yes. Why mince words? People should know in no uncertain terms that liberation is possible. On the other hand, some people will debate such an answer to the point of distraction, so I must point out the following. First, no one — no individual ego-self — becomes enlightened. Second, enlightenment as one thinks about it is just an idea, and clinging to such ideas is the very source of delusion. The truth lies beyond all ideas, beyond all experiences, and beyond all states. I am as I am. And when that is the case, there is nothing to debate.

Q: What does it mean to have no self?

A: What we think of as a self is an aggregate of various things, such as sensations, memories, thoughts, and so on. The coordination and repetition of these things creates the illusion of a separate and independent entity. Through belief in the illusion and identification with it, both of which are also things within the aggregate, one has a self. To have no self is to see directly through all of it to the emptiness within. It is a radical departure from any point of view. It is to recognize no limits. It is to go beyond beyond. The raw ingredients of a self may still be present, but from within, one disappears. The coordination and repetition of the elements no longer creates the illusion of a separate or independent entity. Belief and identification cease. Therefore, from the non-position of no-self, there are no other selves either. There are no separate beings. There are no things or events. In this sense, there are not even any thoughts. All of this is illusion, like the self.

Q: Do you still have preferences?

A: Of course, but I see them for what they are. The personality and its preferences are not utterly destroyed, only the sense that they constitute a separate self. Accordingly some preferences may disappear, but various thoughts and impulses still arise and some preferences may remain. However, there is no identification, no attachment, and no self to which such preferences adhere.

Q: How do you make choices?

A: How does anyone make choices? It's a great mystery if you look into it. You're lying in bed in the morning. At some point you decide to get up. How did you decide? Did you decide to decide? You may have a series of thoughts about it, but at some point you just get up. Enlightened persons don't do things any differently. They just see what's really happening. Choices are made, but there is nobody choosing.

Q: What motivates your actions?

A: Look around you. Everything you see, everything that is unfolding before your eyes ... it's all just happening. The wind in the trees, the waves on the shore, the gathering clouds, the buildings going up, the cars breaking down, it's all motivated by the same process, whatever you want to call it. People are no different. My actions are motivated by that which motivates everything. These words, for example, are like the babbling sounds made by water flowing in a mountain stream. They are nothing more, nothing less.

Q: Can you be distracted?

A: The question presupposes there is something to be distracted from. An ego-self gets wrapped up in thoughts of what it should be doing or thinking. It is bound in time, lost in thoughts — in memories and predictions — reflecting on the myriad things it wants and fears. But whatever is happening *is* what's happening. When you see *that,* there is nothing to be distracted from, nothing to distract you, and no self to be distracted.

Q: How long will it take?

A: It will take no time at all, once it has happened. Before that, it depends on what, how, and from when you are counting. It's not a race, and there is no model to conform to. For there is never a time when you are not your true nature. The ego and individual self are always bound in time, but the eternal Self is always present. To realize it, stop projecting yourself into a past and future. Then time itself will pass away.

Q: If we are already our true nature why make any effort at all?

A: This seems like a contradiction, but let's not make it more complicated than it is. Of course, the truth is always present and always with you. You are always *That.* However, have you realized your own perfection? Until we have realized oneness, some effort is required by the situation we find ourselves in. In short, until effortlessness is realized, effort is unavoidable, so we may as well direct our efforts to the best of our ability, and to the greatest possible ends.

Q: Are spiritual practices necessary?

A: It depends on what you mean by spiritual practices. We are all doing spiritual practices already, whether we know it or not. Everything in life is such a practice. In this sense, some kind of practice is not only necessary but unavoidable. Nevertheless, there is no specific practice that is absolutely necessary. But don't let this be an excuse. It doesn't let anybody off the hook, and dedicated skillful practice can bring one to the doorstep of awakening. So it is more important to remember the first part — that some kind of practice *is* necessary — and engage wholeheartedly with whatever practices appear in the context of your life.

Q: Is a teacher necessary?

A: Again, it depends on what you mean by teacher. If you just mean a teacher in form of a living person, then no, that is not absolutely necessary. Such a teacher could be invaluable. Just to be in the presence of an enlightened teacher can prompt awakening, even if no instruction is given and the effect is beyond our understanding. But all teachers, enlightened or not, can be considered something more than a person. Before realization, something is leading us back to the source of everything. And in the end, something beyond the ego-self is needed for realization to occur. What is it that leads us back and facilitates our return? If that is the teacher we're talking about, then it is absolutely necessary. That teacher can take many forms though, within and without. That teacher is the divine Self, our own true nature. That teacher is the real guru. That teacher is the grace of God.

Q: How will I know if it happens?

A: The truth leaves no room for doubts. Fundamentally you will have no more questions. Your search will be over. You might try looking for something else, something more, something that you felt you once missed, but there will be nothing else, nothing more. It will be clear. You will not be able to imagine anything outside of everything, and everything will be present, here and now.

Q: Will I lose myself?

A: You fear annihilation of the self, but that self has never been anything more than an illusion. In this sense, there is no real self to lose. In awakening you will lose the illusion that you had a self to lose, and in that sense you will lose yourself and the world as you thought it was will end. But have no fear. Nobody will lose it, and in the end there is nothing to lose.

Q: If I really let go, what will keep me from becoming a bad person?

A: That which we fear might take over if we were to let go of the self is nothing other than an aspect of the self. The ego is a tangle of conflicting voices, desires, and impulses. To maintain our conduct and good view of ourselves, some aspects of the self are suppressed while others are encouraged. Letting go does not give these voices free reign, nor must they be constantly held in check, because one sees clearly that none of them were real to begin with. They are all functions of the stories and beliefs that compose the conditioned mind. So you would never be subjected to them any more than you are now. When one really lets go, then love and compassion take their natural course, unhindered by belief in any of the ego's various voices.

Q: Is everything just in my mind?

A: Many people run into this idea of solipsism, that knowledge is limited to what's in your head or your mind. At a certain point this kind of teaching may be appropriate, but all teachings function only as course corrections. The idea that everything is in your head is meant to correct the assumption that some things aren't. But it is not the whole picture, as no teaching or philosophy ever can be. If everything is in your head, you must then ask yourself, in what context does your head appear? If everything is in the mind, from where does the mind arise? Part of the confusion comes from the notion that it is *your* head or *your* mind, let alone that there are heads or minds at all. Solipsism assumes there is an individual self, an owner of heads and minds whose knowledge is limited by them. However, the spiritual path leads to selflessness, not just in thought and action, but in actuality. If questions arise related to solipsism, ask instead: To whom do these questions arise?

In whose mind does any limitation exist? Find the source of the mind, and you will see that the mind itself is an illusion.

Q: Can one be attached to nonattachment?

A: Yes, that's basically nihilism, which is itself a particularly tenacious belief system. It's a kind of trap that can happen when one attempts to approach the truth intellectually but with the ego strong and intact. If one falls into nihilism and can't retreat, take it through to its logical conclusion. The ultimate nihilist must completely negate the self and nihilism as well. And through the deepest darkness there will come the greatest light.

Q: Couldn't enlightenment just be a rare mental state, brain condition, or even a benign psychological disorder?

A: From a particular point of view one could say something like that, but when found, the truth itself is inescapable. No doubts *can* remain. It is not a state, condition, or disorder, for it does not arise within the mind or body. Instead, the mind and body arise within it. The mind and body come and go, whereas it is eternally present. As long as consciousness remains identified with the mind or body, one cannot understand this. When consciousness is liberated from identification, the truth becomes clear, and no doubts can remain. Consider that even now your doubts cannot be sustained, since such thoughts will come and go, and you will have doubts about your doubts. For the enlightened person, all this coming and going, all this mind activity, is transparent. For such persons there is no point of view. They are the truth itself.

BLOCKS AND HANG UPS

If you examine yourself honestly, you will likely find a fair number of physical pains, emotional blocks, and psychological hang-ups that you would rather be without. But trying to work through all your blocks and hang-ups is just like trying to solve all your problems. You will never get to the end of them. Liberation lies not at the end of self improvement, but right here and now.

You may be able to let go of some fears and rid yourself of some pains and anxieties. Others you may have to accommodate and live with for a while. But everything is impermanent. All things pass away, and if you see far enough into yourself, you will see a place untouched by anything. You will see a being that accepts everything, that is all right even when things don't seem all right.

Whatever blocks and hang-ups you think you have that prevent you from letting go, that keep you locked in the past and future or hold you back from awakening, those are not obstructions. To believe you must remove all obstructions is the real obstruction. To think we can keep ourselves apart from the divine with our little hang-ups is the height of presumptuousness.

Everything you can imagine that's holding you back, everything you can think of, is part of this happening, here and now. Nothing can stand outside of it. Everything is divine! Whatever troubles you or causes you doubt — your sore foot, your relationship problems, your past conduct, the feeling that you're not good enough, the thought that it must take a lot of work, the notion that it must be far off — it's all a part of what's happening. These are the very doors to heaven.

It's only the illusion that there is a separate self experiencing these blocks and hang-ups that keeps you from realizing it. But there is no self to be held back. The block you imagine is the flow you seek. Look into what's really happening in this present moment, here and now, and you will see. All separation is illusory.

SEEKING HAPPINESS

Many people these days are obsessed with the pursuit of happiness. All you have to do is look at self-help books, advertisements, and social media to know that this elusive goal of happiness is one of the driving forces in our culture. From all the excitement, hype, and activity, one could imagine that if happiness ever really arrived, people would be sorely disappointed. What would they do now?

This is the point I would like to make about happiness. Aside from a few necessities, what really is needed? One might argue that for true happiness, even the necessities aren't needed. So why are so many people, especially affluent people, still seeking it?

Seeking happiness is one of the simplest and most effective of all worldly traps. And because of this, an examination of it can be quite instructive.

If you want to be happy, if you desire happiness, you are in fact saying you are an unhappy person. Okay, fair enough, perhaps you feel unhappy. But at least ask yourself: What comes first, the desire for happiness or the feeling of unhappiness? Or do they perhaps arise mutually?

When we seek happiness, we usually place it somewhere in the future. After all, if we thought it were here now, why would we seek it? So we imagine we will find it when certain conditions are met, and our culture is exceptionally good at reinforcing this idea. You will be happy when you get the right job, when you meet the right person, when you get in shape, when you lose weight, when your back stops hurting, when you make so much money, when you get the house, when you get the car, when you have a child, when the child is grown up, when the laws are changed, when the environment is saved, and so on and so on. There is no end to the conditions one can imagine. And because of that, they will never be met.

As long as you seek happiness through an arrangement of circumstances, you will always be seeking it. You will never be able to arrange everything just right, so all the conditions have been met. Even if you could momentarily arrange everything so it was perfect — even just good — what then? How long could that last? Soon you would be seeking your happiness in the past. *Oh, if only things could be like they were,* and so on.

By placing happiness somewhere in the past or future, it can only ever be imaginary. In the present moment, aside from occasional fleeting pleasures, future happiness will still be thought of as residing in the future. And once habituated to this way of thinking, it perpetuates itself. If former conditions for happiness have been met, new condition will be invented to explain why happiness still seems elusive. The ordinary mind can play this game forever, for it will always keep the reified ego and the gratification of the self in the spotlight of attention.

If you can, stop seeking all together. Forget about happiness and unhappiness. But while craving persists, if you must seek happiness, seek it now, in this present moment, in what is actually happening. Do not seek it in the past or future. There is no past or future. Turn the floodlight of your awareness on this ever-present moment, regardless of circumstances, and find your happiness now.

Become Like a Child Again

Most adults approach every situation in life with a whole history of preconceptions, thoughts, fears, and desires. When we do this, we are trying to manage and control ourselves, our environment, and our experience through our thoughts to such a degree that we rarely see what's really happening *as* it's happening. We operate from a multitude of predictions of what might be about to happen and memories of what we think just happened. We constantly judge ourselves, others, and situations, and we get wrapped up in emotional responses to our thoughts and judgments. Because of this, we are often filled with some form of fear and anxiety, and are rarely present in the moment.

One of the ways you can start to experience a different way of approaching life is to deliberately adopt a childlike perspective on things. Cultivate a kind of naivety, perhaps even a kind of stupidity, in your daily life. What do I mean by this? It's not that you forget your memories of past experience, but you don't rely on them. You drop all unnecessary pre-conceptions, predictions, and judgments. And you drop all thoughts about conforming to some social expectation or any ideas of appropriate response. Expect neither good nor bad outcomes. Just see what happens. This is a good attitude in any practice, and in everyday life.

Let's say you have social anxiety and have to go to a party, or maybe you're talking to a friend who reveals their mother just died, or you're going to see your boss for a review of your job performance. Instead of predicting how the interaction will go, based on prior experience or your own ideas, admit that you really don't know what's going to happen, and be open to whatever experience comes out of it. During any interaction, instead of worrying if you are saying the right things or showing the right emotions and reactions, just take in what's happening, be present and receptive with no pressure on yourself to do or say anything. Instead of judging the situation, go into it with nothing more than kindness for others and curiosity to see what will unfold.

Try not to be swept up and lost in personal stories, judgments, or emotions — whether your own or another person's. It's not always easy. You'll have to humble yourself and risk appearing actually stupid, weak, insensitive, or awkward. But the more you can approach life with this childlike innocence, this intelligent stupidity, the less anxious and afraid you will be. Freed from the taxing rush of thoughts and emotions, you will find yourself more perceptive, more honest, and more compassionate. Paradoxically, by giving up grasping at some personal sense of control, you will have greater influence over situations. That is because you will have stopped fighting with yourself. Give up illusory sources of power and you will start to experience what true power is.

In Zen and Japanese martial arts, this is very similar to the idea of *mushin,* commonly translated as "no mind." By having no fixed thoughts and not relying on any particular technique or point of view, by not grasping at any hope of victory and not holding any fear of defeat, the master leaves no opening. He stands there, completely present and free. By not being ready for something, he is ready for anything. This is likened to water in a barrel. It sits there completely still, at rest, but if you put a hole anywhere in the barrel, the water flows out immediately, without any hesitation, without any effort. And really, all of life can be like that.

WATCHER OF THOUGHTS

Abide in the awareness that lies beyond thought. Observe your thoughts as they arise. Just try at first to identify them as thoughts. This will give you some space in which to cease identifying with them. Watch them and see where they go, but don't get caught up in them. If you become lost in thought, gently return to the awareness in which you can be the watcher of your thoughts.

If you don't get caught up in or attached to your thoughts, they will cease to be a problem, and fewer unnecessary thoughts will arise. Eventually their importance will diminish greatly. You will see them arise out of nowhere, run their course, and disappear from consciousness. Thoughts are like shooting stars in the gravity of your awareness.

Where I live, there is a beautiful park that runs along the river, with a paved path through grassy fields dotted with maples and Douglas-fir. It's a wonderful place to walk. If you walk far enough, you come to a highway overpass. One day I stopped there and stood looking at all the cars zooming by overhead. Many went one way, many the other, and there was no end to them.

This is the place to which you've come. Watch the cars going this way and that. As soon as one goes by one way, another goes by the other way. If you latch onto one and start thinking about it, you are lost. You will start wondering who is in that car, and where are they going, and what is their final destination, but you will never reach the end of the journey. You are, after all, still standing in the park, here and now.

Watch your thoughts go by, like cars on the overpass. At some point, you may realize they're going nowhere — just this way and that, round and round. And when you've had enough, just turn and walk away, back into the beauty of the park, along a path where autumn leaves drift through the air, and you notice the sound of the river once more.

Unmoored Consciousness

The issue with the ego is not that you have one. It has never been anything more than an illusion. The same is true for the body. The issue is really one of identification. Through identification with the ego-self, with subject and objects, mind and body, with thoughts, voices and images, we separate ourselves off from our true nature. And this feeling of separateness engenders certain beliefs that reinforce the identification process.

To liberate consciousness, the cycle of identification must be broken. Is there any way you can do this? Ultimately, no, because the doing you is a function of identification, and simply put, a knife cannot cut itself. There's no way around this. But perhaps there are hints and insights that push one in the direction of liberation. Certain trains of thought, meditation practices, and physical practices may reveal the identification process, consciously or unconsciously, and help prepare the way.

Consider, just as an example, the little or not-so-little voice in your head. It is constantly telling you things about yourself, as if you wouldn't know. It is always telling you what to do, as if you wouldn't just do it. And to make matters worse, it insists on arguing with you. Now, I ask you, in all seriousness, who are you arguing with when you argue with yourself like that?

During meditation, when the mind is quiet, if you pay attention you can see thoughts and images, and hear voices as they arise and disappear. From where do they come? To where do they go? Where are you in all this? Don't think about it. You cannot answer with another thought, another image or voice. Perceive it directly.

Examine the feeling you have in your body. There is a certain pattern of tension or energy that is present. This is what it feels like to be you. But *is* it you? You may notice more tension than is necessary for whatever it is you're doing. Why is that? When you anticipate or experience pain, you may tense up even more. Does it help? What are you holding on to? When you feel sorry for yourself, who is it that's feeling sorry … and for whom?

Generally, when we seek to change some pattern of thought, behavior, or tension, the process of identification is just redirected. This, for example, is the idea behind cognitive behavior therapy, physical therapy, addiction recovery, self-help, and so on. Although one may cease identifying with one pattern, it is accomplished by replacing it with another pattern. Hopefully it is a healthier pattern, but the identification cycle continues unbroken.

Maybe, however, in such a shift, you can see the identification process as it's happening. In seeing it clearly, the process of identification is deprived of power. It cannot complete itself. It is like a magic trick, and once you see how it's done, the illusion no longer works. So now, what would happen if the whole process just stopped? What would happen if you were cut loose, if you were freed from all manner of identification?

GLIMPSING BEYOND

At some point in your life you may have — or already have had — a transcendental flash of insight. This could happen during a spiritual practice, in an extreme circumstance, or simply in the course of everyday life. How should we interpret and understand such experiences?

Many people will dismiss them as anomalous altered states of consciousness or hallucinations of some sort. Some will interpret them as a divine or supernatural occurrences. Such experiences can vary in length and degree of intensity, and depending on your background and the context, could be met with terror at one extreme and ecstasy at the other.

Throughout my life, I had a number of experiences that I only now recognize as partial glimpses into awakening. But while those happenings seemed extraordinary at the time, I did not understand their full significance. Nor did any actual realization occur. Nor did I imagine in any way that it was possible to go beyond such temporary states to a complete and permanent transformation of consciousness.

Of course, not all extraordinary or spiritual experiences are glimpses into awakening, and these glimpses are definitely not awakening itself. Some experiences — and even some thoughts — are simply extraordinary. While they may point toward something greater than we understand, or suggest consciousness plays a role in our perception, they are not direct glimpses into the nature of awakening any more than everyday experiences are.

Without an enlightened teacher to advise you about an experience, you are left on your own to wonder at the significance of whatever has happened. There's nothing wrong with that, as long as you don't jump to self-aggrandizing conclusions or start inventing wild metaphysical explanations. There is nothing wrong with simply not knowing. In fact, it's likely that this unknowing will bring you closest to the truth.

Do not cling to any experience you have had, nor crave the extraordinary. In the case of an actual gnostic flash or a partial awakening, the ego and conceptual awareness has momentarily receded to reveal a glimpse of primordial consciousness. As the ego and conceptual thinking returns, they will try to make sense of what has happened in terms of the ego and various worldly and spiritual concepts. In an effort to incorporate the experience into conceptual awareness, the ego may dismiss it or cling to it, claiming it as its own in some gross or subtle way.

Remember that although the ego cannot become enlightened, it can certainly pretend to be, and it can create all kinds of wild stories to keep itself at the center of attention. Know that genuine awakening is not an experience that comes and goes. It is an abiding awareness, an undeniable recognition, a complete realization, totally fulfilling, but it cannot be grasped or attained by any individual self.

Stranger Things

I want to discuss a few other types of strange experiences that people may have had, and what to make of them, if anything. I have rarely spoken of the unusual experiences I had before awakening, but I think they are important to mention because I suspect they are not as uncommon as one might think. And while these experiences may open the mind by suggesting the true nature of reality is not how it appears, they are also very easily misunderstood.

There are a whole range of strange experiences that can occur, in meditation or out of it, during sleep or while awake in everyday life. These include out-of-body experiences, sleep paralysis, encounters with angelic, demonic, or alien beings, encounters with ghosts or other spirits, visits to other realms, déjà vu, lucid dreaming, death dreams, spiritual dreams, and near-death experiences. And at one point or another, starting around the age of fourteen, I've experienced most of these phenomena.

I once saw myself through the eyes of seagull as it flew by where I sat on the clifftops of an ocean shoreline. I once felt the sun, moon, and earth turning in their orbits. And I have awoken within countless dreams to explore the landscape of sleep with a conscious mind.

At one point in my life, I learned to self-induce out-of-body experiences. During one experiment, I was taken by an invisible, angelic being to an in-between realm, where I saw on the strange horizon a brilliant white light radiating with bliss. This I recognized as the light of God shining out of heaven. What indescribable longing I felt for it! What heartbreak when it set like the sun below the horizon and the angel returned me to my body.

During bouts of sleep paralysis, I have seen a variety of demonic and alien beings emanating a palpable and terrifying aura of evil. During such episodes, I could not wake, nor speak, nor scream. One time I sat bolt upright, opened my eyes, and for several seconds I could not see the room in front of me. Wide awake, I could see nothing but the horrific vision before my eyes.

These types of experiences can be so vivid, so real, so terrifying or beautiful or profound that it is almost impossible not to ascribe some meaning to them. In the moment, it is difficult not to entertain the possibility that some external supernatural force could be at work. I found it hard to accept that they had no significance, but I doubted that I was being visited by actual angels and demons, at least in the way such things are usually imagined. Yet the experiences were what they were.

Most spiritual traditions seem to agree that such phenomena, while not insignificant, can be a distraction, and fall far from the realization of actual awakening. I would have to agree. These experiences are, like everything else, forms arising in consciousness. I am the angel and the demon and the lord. In the radiant light is an image of the ultimate realization and an absolute longing for the divine. In the evil beings are all the fears of the ego personified.

I would say even the wildest reports of drug-induced experiences also fall into this same area of interpretation. Although some drug experiences might be helpful in opening the mind to new possibilities, drugs can also harm the body and mind, as well as create physical or psychological addictions, thus decreasing, not increasing the possibility of awakening. The awakened state is not an altered state. It is your original state. From any drug-induced experience you will always come down, moving from one distortion to another, without ever reaching the truth.

Of course, all such experiences can have symbolic significance and present profound opportunities to understand oneself. But unless you recognize consciousness itself, they are still just experiences and could drive one deeper into delusion if misunderstood as the objects of an egocentric story.

Nothing Special

In a way, the truth is ultimately nothing special. After all, it's always what's actually happening right now. In this sense, it is totally ordinary — so ordinary, in fact, that most people miss it entirely. It is so ordinary that it might seem like a disappointment when I say it's right in front of you, but it is.

This is why the Zen master says things like "Eat your soup!" and leaves it at that. Stop all your seeking already! Why do you hope for somebody else to reveal the secret to you? Exactly what kind of an explanation are you waiting for? The soup is right there.

You see, there is something amazing when you really see this nothing special. People are so accustomed to everyday experience that they do not see how incredible it all is, how unlikely, how inexplicable, how strange, how beautiful, how divine.

At last, a Zen poem puts it this way:

> Miraculous power and marvelous activity —
> Drawing water and hewing wood!

When you see the truth, this miraculous power and marvelous activity is revealed in everything. There is no need to seek anything special. This nothing special is all you need.

Seeing is Being

Throughout these writings, I have said frequently that you must see it for yourself. I am trying to express the necessity of one's own inquiry, but such phrasing can be misleading. So at the risk of repeating what I have already said, I want to try one last time to be clear about this.

First, "seeing" here represents the entire field of total perception. But the very phrase "see it for yourself" could inadvertently reinforce subject-object duality. This will be misleading if you expect that you will at last see some special thing, something separate from yourself.

Instead, when you recognize it, you will realize, once and for all, that you *are* it. That which you see is that which is seeing. In other words, that which is before you *is* what you are. That is your true nature. There is nothing other than that. In Sanskrit it is said, *Tat tvam asi,* meaning "That thou art." And this is what you must see for yourself. Fundamentally, you are what is.

I don't think I can be any clearer than that.

You Cannot Escape

You may think you are seeking the truth, seeking enlightenment, or seeking God, but all your seeking is really just an attempt to escape. That is why you cannot find what you seek. Even if you're not seeking, you're still trying to escape some other way — through hedonism, concepts and theories, metaphors and systems of thought, religions, drugs, self-improvement, wealth, power, and so on. It's all an attempt to escape from what is, to escape from yourself, to escape from the world. In a way, you are actually trying to escape from the truth, escape from enlightenment, escape from God.

There is no escape!

You can pretend all you want, for as long as you want. There's nothing wrong with that. But you cannot really escape your true nature. You cannot be separate from what's happening. Not a single thing can be outside of everything. And there is no way *not* to be exactly who and what you are in this present moment. There is no way not to be doing that which you are doing right now. There is no way not to think the thoughts you think, or not to choose the choices you make.

It's all happening now.

This is it.

Whatever you do, you cannot escape it.

So put aside all thoughts of attaining to some other realm, of reaching greatness, of finding future satisfaction. Put aside all thoughts of success, of improving yourself, or figuring out the universe. That's all an impossible dream of escaping that which is right before you in this very moment.

If you can accept yourself in this situation completely, along with everything that entails, then you can accept everything. Beyond that, no self will remain. You are already one with all that is. Stop trying to escape, and the doors of heaven will open to you.

THE TEACHING

In writing, I have tried to introduce as few new concepts as possible. I've used existing vocabulary wherever I could, while trying not to get the words too mixed up. But I will indulge myself by concluding with this idea of the Teaching. It is, of course, only an idea, but it may be a useful one that is not tied directly to similar ideas in various specific traditions.

The Teaching is the abstract selfless means by which truth is revealed. It may act through persons and books, through mediation and self-inquiry, through dreams and visions, and even through objects, actions, and events.

The ultimate purpose of the Teaching is not to explain how things are, nor to create or elicit belief in any conceptual model or metaphysical idea. All these things, if adhered to, if clung to, will only continue the cycle of delusion.

The ultimate purpose of the Teaching is to prompt awakening. Its end is not understanding as it is commonly thought, nor subservience to any thought or system of thoughts, but rather complete liberation through realization of the truth.

Sometimes a seemingly evasive answer is actually the true Teaching. An explanation may seem to contradict itself without ultimately contradicting itself. Remember that what the Teaching is about is truly beyond words, and always will be. Ultimately, you have to realize the truth for yourself.

If one does not awaken immediately, the Teaching simply points toward it. If one insists on perpetuating problems, the Teaching shows the impossibility of any real and lasting solution. If one holds on to concepts and ideas, the Teaching demolishes them. If one clings to attachments, the Teaching shows what and how and where. If one continues in folly, the Teaching encourages folly until wisdom dawns.

PART IV

PRACTICES

As the water flows,
You flow.
As the rock abides,
You abide.
As the tree sways,
You sway.
Like the wind,
You come and go,
Here and there,
Leaving no trace
of your passing.

THE PURPOSE OF PRACTICE

My own spiritual journey was not marked by any clear direction or tradition. In many ways, aside from forays into Eastern and Western religions, this journey was largely a secret, even to myself. This was true especially toward the end, when I had given up all hope of discovering any truth, improving myself, or attaining any goal. That being said, over the years I did engage in practices such as meditation, martial arts, even devotion and prayer. And I discovered later some things I experimented with, such as lucid dreaming, have specific practices. So while I was not outwardly a dedicated spiritual practitioner, these practices no doubt played a role in my eventual awakening. Likewise, some dedicated practice could play a role in yours.

My intention is not to prescribe a specific or hermetic system of spiritual practices. Such systems exist if you desire one, but no practice is absolutely necessary for awakening, nor can guarantee it. However, there are practices that may prepare the way, and all of them are blessings in their own right, for by and large they promote health, happiness, and well-being, even for those who are not seeking enlightenment. Therefore, I want to suggest a number of ideas and exercises. The practices described are places to begin. They could, in fact, form a lifetime of study, but exhaustive instructions are beyond the scope of this book. In any case, you will have to discover for yourself where they lead.

Before going on, it's important to understand something about the purpose and principle of such exercises. Although I will suggest a variety of practices that seem mental, physical, or spiritual in nature, keep in mind that there are really no distinctions between these categories. Those are all just ideas we have. Practices may act in a multiplicity of ways and have a variety of benefits, but in this context all these practices share a similar purpose.

The purpose of such exercises is to serve as a catalyst for inquiry, to point out desires and attachments, to disrupt identification with the ego and conceptual thought, and to create situations where one might recognize impermanence, understand oneself, and realize one's true nature. The basic principle at work is to push at the boundaries of the self and its conceptual framework, in one way or another. The goal of any practice is never the success or improvement of the ego-self, but rather to see through the ego altogether.

Whatever practices you undertake, the ego will continually adapt, re-arranging and re-identifying with a conceptual framework to maintain the sense of self. However, even if the shell of the ego does not crack readily or permanently, a beneficial practice will create healthier, more compassionate, and less self-obsessed people … and ultimately, people more prepared for awakening.

These practices are not unique. Many can be found in various traditions, and I have adapted them from my exposure to different types of meditation and health practices. You can seek out more detailed instruction if you wish. Most of the exercises are fairly simple, but they contain great depth, and there are many possible variations. A desire for immediate gratification is the response of the ego and an opportunity for insight even before you begin. It's better to approach the practices as an end unto themselves. Even if you don't realize enlightenment, profound and lasting benefits can arise from a committed regular practice.

How to Practice

Whatever practices you undertake, there are several points I would like to make regarding *how* to practice. Consider the following ideas when thinking about your approach to practice: intention, contrast, consistency, inquiry, and responsibility. I'll discuss the importance of each idea below.

Examine your intention for undertaking any practice. Are you really trying to find a way to let go? Do you really want to discover the truth about yourself, no matter what it is? Or are you just trying to get something for yourself? Are you just trying to acquire something — some mastery, some credential, or some sort of experience. Your true intent could play a decisive role in how your practice unfolds.

There is a sense in which practices function at a super-conscious level. With intention, they create a way of allowing the cycle of identification to break, or of giving permission to yourself to let go. But there is little point in talking about this aspect of practice too much since, aside from any conscious intention, it is not within our conscious awareness. It's enough to say intention matters.

The idea of noticing contrast is one way to evaluate practices. Things were one way, and now they're a different way. For example, *I was anxious and now I'm calm.* This is something the ordinary mind might deem progress if the new way is deemed better than the old way. But the paradox of spiritual practice is that there can be no progress toward the absolute. It is always present. So setting aside the idea of progress for now, stick with creating and noticing contrast. It's a lot less daunting and more to the point.

Why contrast? Simply put, contrast in all forms is what makes things intelligible and what creates opportunities for transcending duality. Contrast provides stimulus for inquiry into identification, the self, objects, the body, impermanence, and so on.

Practicing consistently is the key to creating contrast. You can't do everything, so pick one or two practices and do them consistently for at least two weeks. Ten minutes every day is better than one hour twice a week. The idea is to allow for a noticeable change to take place. For example, if your practice is trying to touch your toes and you try once, and then try again four days later, and then again in a month, you will not notice any change. And your toe-touching practice will be pretty uninteresting. If you do it morning and night, every day for two weeks, I guarantee you will notice changes.

Now, consistency may be enough if you're just looking to see some beneficial changes to the mind or body. And noticing contrast may be enough if you're just looking to feel like you're making progress. But if you're seeking the truth, inquiry is essential to your practice. In fact, every practice should have its roots in inquiry. Ask questions and seek the truth, even in something as simple as touching your toes. Be attentive and observe what's really happening. In this way your practice will become self-informed and self-directed. You will see where you need to go next, instead of just following someone else's instructions.

This brings us to the notion of responsibility. You are responsible for your own practice and where it takes you. Any instruction you receive is only a starting place. A teacher may point, but you have to look. You have to do the real work, and nobody can do it for you.

Cautionary Words

Practices actually have little to do with enlightenment when it gets down to it. They are more about processing, working with, understanding, breaking down, and seeing through delusions. They are more about removing obstacles to realization than realization itself. The truth is always present. There is no need to practice it. However, many things may obscure it from your vision, and if you wish to see through these obstacles, some work is probably necessary.

A practice is like an intervention or a medicine. That's why there are so many possible practices. Depending on the person and the obstacle, one practice may be more effective than another at removing it. Since it's often difficult to know what the obstacles are, a fair amount of experimentation with practices is helpful. And you will discover all kinds of wonderful things along the way.

Practices can be beneficial, healthy, rewarding, and provide pleasant and interesting sensations and experiences. That's all well and good. But if you are seeking the truth, don't lose sight of your ongoing inquiry. If you simply follow instructions but never think for yourself, you're wasting time. Don't become complacent or satisfied with your practice, or for that matter, with any explanation or story about the spiritual world. Practices may assist you, but the truth lies beyond all practice.

It's good to be clear about this. You have to do the work, but in the end everything will be transcended. So don't hang on to anything along the way. Practices themselves can be a trap if you're not careful. And all the technicalities, explanations, and lofty ideas thrown about, not to mention the hopes and fears, can be like throwing gasoline on the fire of the mind and the ego. Don't fall for it. Just do the work. Be clear headed in your approach. Enjoy the benefits of practice, but don't mistake a practice or an experience for realization.

Beginning Meditation

If I had to recommend only one practice, it would be meditation. Some of you may have extensive meditation experience and others may not really know what it is. There are many different types of meditation with specialized instructions, but the basics are pretty simple. Just sit there being aware of what is.

The various instructions for meditation can be useful. But to start, try just not doing anything for a short period of time, and be aware of what's around you and whatever is going on. Do you notice things about your surroundings? Do you become anxious? Do you want to move? Do you become self-conscious? Do you feel silly? Just observe, whatever comes up. There is no right or wrong outcome. You can't fail. Even if you stop after ten seconds for some reason, that is what you've observed. Even if it seems you have observed nothing, observe that.

Expect no result. There is absolutely no goal to the exercise except to be aware of what's happening. Make no judgment about success or failure, or about regularity or discipline. If you find yourself having expectations or judgments, observe that. Observe, observe, observe.

Eventually, you don't have to be sitting or even in one place to do this. Meditation can happen anywhere, while walking or running or waiting for the bus, even while dreaming, since the essence is just giving your attention to what is before you.

Whatever type of formal meditation practice you do from here on out, you can always fall back on this basic idea. Just be aware of what is. My aim here is not to provide guided meditations or exhaustive instructions. If you feel you need these, seek them out. There are plenty of great resources. That being said, I will describe several specific exercises to get you started, and they may provide you with everything you need.

Sitting Logistics

Don't obsess over technical details. Your body position is not critical, but try practicing with upright posture. Not only will good spinal alignment have health benefits, but it will help create an optimal combination of relaxation and attention. If you're flexible and can get into a stable cross-legged sitting position on the floor or a cushion, that's great. If not, there is nothing wrong with sitting on a chair, though it's best to sit upright without leaning back.

Once you're seated, take a few deep breaths. Inhale through the nose and exhale out the mouth. With each inhale, find any excessive tension in the body or mind. With each exhale, release the excess tension while maintaining your form. After a few deep breaths, breathe normally, inhaling and exhaling through the nose.

You can meditate with the eyes open or closed. If you close the eyes, allow them to shut lightly as you exhale your last deep breath and resume normal breathing. If you keep the eyes open, allow them to gaze ahead, slightly downward, with no fixed focal point.

Take a few moments to settle in by opening your awareness to the entire field of perception. Take in whatever sights, sounds, smells, and sensations are present, without analysis. Just note all these sensations, allowing each one to carry you deeper into your perceptions.

Once you've settled in, you'll be ready to engage in any specific meditation practice, or just continue sitting with open awareness. A meditation session can last as long as you like, but aiming for somewhere between ten and twenty minutes is a good start. Eventually, you can increase the time for one sitting to between thirty minutes and an hour.

Whatever practices you engage in, toward the end of the session, allow some time to just let the mind go. Let it do whatever it wants. Do not guide it, restrain it, or focus it in any way. Just see what happens without doing anything at all. Make no distinction, no discrimination, no judgment, and no choice with regard to the direction or contents of the mind.

As you conclude any session, bring your attention gently back to the body and the environment around you. Open your eyes as you inhale, if they aren't already open, and notice how you feel. Try to carry this feeling into your everyday life.

Regular practice is best, but there's no need to be fanatical. There are times for light mediation and times for going deep into it. Treat your practice as a kind of experiment, an enjoyable kind of play. If you miss a regular session, or a week, or even twenty years, no judgment is necessary — or helpful. Just start practicing again.

Sustaining Attention

While meditating, turn your awareness to the breath and keep your attention on each successive inhale and exhale. If you find your attention has wavered or you've become distracted by thoughts, gently return your awareness to the breath. At the beginning you may find it helpful to count your breaths, one to ten and repeat. Eventually, you can just follow the ongoing stream of the breath.

Don't judge your performance. Make a sincere effort, but with no regard for results. Noticing you've become distracted and gently returning the attention to the breath is as much the exercise as keeping the awareness on the breath. Yes, it's really this simple. No, you can't win or lose.

The breath is a convenient object for sustaining attention and has many benefits, but if you prefer to focus on something else, that's fine. Some people repeat a word, a mantra, or a prayer. Some choose an object such as a candle, a mandala, a stone, or a waterfall. There's no reason why you can't explore the practice with all these things. In fact, I suggest you do. There really are no rules, and while there are meditation techniques, actual meditation is not a technique.

Once you've spent some sessions sustaining attention, start looking at distractions in a little more detail. Whenever distracted by a thought, an emotion, or some sensation, just identify it as such, and gently return your attention to the breath. If a thought distracts you, note that it is a thought. If an emotion distracts you, note that it is an emotion. If you are distracted by a noise, a pain, hunger, or any other sensations, just note that it is a sensation.

Don't follow any further train of thoughts regarding these things. Just note what they are and return your attention to the breath, or whatever object you are focusing on. You might notice that identifying distractions is just another thought, or that the breath is just another sensation. That's all right. Just try to keep yourself from getting caught up in any train of thoughts.

Observing Thoughts

In this meditation exercise, observe your thoughts as they come and go, appearing and disappearing in consciousness. Observe how they take shape, arise, change, and subside again. Your thoughts themselves and the silence they come out of are the object of this meditation.

Just watch, and see if you can detect the moment a thought appears in consciousness. There it is. Continue to watch it as it is happening. See if you can catch the moment it disappears from consciousness. Now it's gone. It has returned from whence it came. Now wait for the next one. Suddenly a new thought arises, or a repetition of the previous thought. Watch that one too.

Again, try not to get caught up in any particular thought or train of thoughts. But when you do get caught — and you will — watch how it happens. Observe how the mind latches onto a thought and identifies with it. See how new, related thoughts arise, creating a train of thoughts that, in turn, are also grasped at and believed.

Watch all your thoughts, whatever they are, as they come and go. See how some go this way and others that way. Just watch them go by, like cars on an overpass, or like clouds drifting by in a clear sky. Note that none can last, even troublesome, persistent thoughts. Even the most obsessive, judgmental, neurotic thoughts disappear if you watch them long enough. None can endure in the pure light of your awareness.

There are many variations of this practice. Instead of observing thoughts, for example, you can observe emotions by quietly attending to present emotions or by conjuring various emotions and watching them run their course. See what happens when you gaze directly at them. This practice can lead to an understanding of how to transform negativity. You can also observe sensations by focusing on a type of sensation, such as sound, sight, taste and smell, bodily sensations, and so on. In each case, try to observe how phenomena arise, change, transform, and disappear.

OPEN AWARENESS

This fundamental meditation practice focuses on cultivating awareness of the entire field of perception, ultimately without exercising any discrimination or choice.

During meditation, although you're just sitting there, you'll notice a lot is happening in and around you once you start paying attention. There's so much going on, in fact, that before practicing open awareness, you might start with some selective awareness. For a few moments, focus your awareness on sounds, then sight, then taste and smell, then bodily sensations. Finally, focus your awareness on observing any thoughts and emotions that are present. You can practice these all selectively with sustained attention, as described already.

While observing, try not to mentally label or analyze any phenomenon that arises. Allow everything that arises to appear or disappear without resistance or grasping. This is especially important with thoughts and emotions, when the tendency is to get involved with them, incorporate them into personal narratives, and connect them to more thoughts. Just let them go.

Once you've practiced awareness of these phenomena individually, try opening your awareness to the entire field of perception. The feeling is one of deep quiescence. The awareness is broad and expansive, in which various phenomena arise and subside. Again, allow everything that arises to appear or disappear without resistance or grasping. Do not guide your attention in any way whatsoever. Just abide in awareness itself.

Notice that this is similar to instruction given earlier on simply letting the mind do whatever it wants. But now we've really opened the awareness in order to take in the entire field of perception without grasping or resistance. Still, all you're doing is being aware of whatever arises, whether it seems to be inside or outside the body or the mind.

This can form the backbone of an ongoing meditation practice, in and out of formal sitting, and can spread throughout your entire life. Let everything take its own course. Just be present in this ever-changing moment. Anything that arises or falls away only takes you deeper into it.

SEEING NOTHING

The last meditation exercise I'll describe focuses on re-acquainting yourself with nothing. Instead of keeping your awareness on the breath during mediation, or on a candle or word, or even on your thoughts, or any other thing or object, keep your attention on nothing. Stop all your thoughts, and gaze into emptiness, aware of nothing.

How do you do this? How can you be aware of nothing? You can't do it by focusing on the idea of nothing, nor by thinking about it. That's just turning nothing into a thing. Instead, simply eliminate everything that is a thing from your awareness. What remains is nothing.

One way to start is by closing your eyes. Even if you start this way, let no thing stand out in your awareness. And remember, darkness, lights, shapes, thoughts, are all things. If you leave the eyes open, do not focus on anything within the field of vision. You're seeing, but not seeing *things*. Let the eyes fall nowhere and on no thing. If the mind begins to discern or focus on a thing in the field of vision — be it an object, a color, a texture, a shape, whatever — gently return your awareness to nothing.

Whenever any thought arises, be it random or prompted by a feeling or a sensation, gently return your attention to nothing. Be very gentle about this, so you don't rebound onto something else, make a thing out of nothing, or have a cascading series of thoughts. Be so gentle, in fact, that it is not like doing anything. It is more like simply abandoning the thought, even as it arises, and eventually before it even takes shape.

Thoughts, feelings, sensations … treat them all the same way. Give no energy to them. Abandon all distinctions, even as they arise. Notice that the instructions are very similar to sustaining attention on an object such as the breath or a candle, but in this case there is no object to sustain the attention. The practice is just pure letting go, pure non-attachment.

This can be an intense practice and it may be best to meditate for a only few concentrated minutes at first. Also, it is not necessarily meant as a long-term practice. Stopping all thought is not the end goal. And as already stated, success in any practice is not the goal either. That being said, occasionally engaging in such a practice can be helpful and instructive, by either a failure to stop your thoughts, or by revealing an awareness that lies beyond thought.

Breath Exploration

Because breathing can seem both voluntary and involuntary, it can be a link between the mind and the body, and studying it directly can yield insight into the ego, its boundaries, and the nature of the self. Use the following two exercises as a way to inquire into the nature of the breath and self.

For the first exercise, observe your breath from any position, consciously and voluntarily, then unconsciously and involuntarily. Start by inhaling and exhaling consciously, controlling the beginning and the ending of each inhale, pause, and exhale. Then let go of conscious breath control and attempt to observe the breath happening all on its own. Make no decision about when to inhale, when to pause, when to exhale, or how long each segment of the cycle lasts. Just let the whole thing happen on its own, but watch it happening.

Next, try switching back and forth between voluntary and involuntary breathing modes every five or ten breaths. Notice that during voluntary breathing it seems as if *you* are breathing, but during involuntary breathing it almost seems as if something else is breathing. What is that? As you become more proficient, try to find the boundary between the voluntary and the involuntary by making your control over voluntary breathing more and more quiet, more and more subtle. At what point does it become involuntary? What distinguishes one from the other?

A variation of this exercise would be to voluntarily breathe into various parts of the body. Try to direct the breath into different parts of the lungs, as well as to push the feeling of the breath into the legs or arms, the back or head, and so on. Then, during the involuntary breath cycles, try to see where the breath goes all on its own. Again, explore the boundary between the voluntary and involuntary.

BREATH SUSPENSION

For the second exercise, lie down on the floor. Inhale naturally and exhale about three-fourths of the air, so the body reaches a neutral tension level or neutral pressure in relation to the outside air. Then suspend your breath. Hold your breath like this and observe any reactions as the breath hold gets longer. Where does tension accumulate? What feelings and thoughts do you have? What happens to your pulse and blood pressure? What sensations do you have?

A word of caution may be needed here. Don't get too fanatical about how long you hold your breath. It is possible to voluntarily hold your breath long enough to pass out, and I am not recommending this. Unless you fall or are underwater it isn't particularly dangerous; you will automatically start breathing again. But while this fact in and of itself may be instructive, there's no need to test it out.

In any case, holding your breath longer and longer is a bit of a trap. Holding the breath is just an opportunity to see contrast and conduct inquiry. The point is not only to go longer, but to become sensitive earlier and to smaller and smaller changes.

At some point, you may notice you seem to be having a kind of argument with yourself. On the one side the mind says *You can hold your breath longer,* and on the other side it says *Breathe, breathe, breathe!* The intensity of this argument can reach a fevered pitch, until finally, sometimes spontaneously, without any real decision or voluntary control, you start to breathe again.

You're not done yet, though. Stressing the system is only half the exercise. Recovery is just as important. Breathe in through the nose and out the mouth until you have returned yourself to a relaxed baseline, particularly with regard to heart rate and breathing. Note any feelings, thoughts, and sensations during recovery. When you have restored yourself fully, consider the following questions as a starting point for inquiry: In the midst of holding your breath, when that internal argument was going on, who exactly were you arguing with? Who won? In the midst of recovery, who or what was being restored? And who was doing the restoration?

Breath Check

Throughout the day, your breathing is happening on a largely unconscious level. That doesn't mean it's functioning as well as it could be. The problems of the ego and all its attachments can have a detrimental effect on thoughts, emotions, tension, and breathing.

In general, breathing should be free, easy, and continuous — inhaling and exhaling through the nose. For more focused and efficient breathing, breathe in through the nose and out the mouth. As activity increases the breath rate increases, and so on. But when fear, stress, or disturbing thoughts and emotions arise, the normal pattern is interrupted. Sometimes fear and stress are so constant that over time the normal breathing pattern enters a state of chronic disruption.

Breath interruptions can be subtle or quite drastic. People may hold or alter their breath when writing their name, getting up from a chair, or opening a door. And of course, breathing is affected when people are scared, injured, in pain, or during increased activity. Any interruption to breathing puts additional stresses on the body and mind. Many interruptions are psychological, fear and thought based, and rooted in the conditioned ego. They have immediate detrimental effects and long-term effects.

The following practice is quite simple, but done regularly, it offers profound insights into how you think, move, and react to various situations and changes in the total environment. Periodically, just check in with your breathing. You could do this on a schedule, or by making a mental note to observe your breathing as much as possible throughout the day.

Take particular care to observe your breathing whenever any stresses or strains are present, be they emotional, physical, or psychological. Whenever you notice your breathing is irregular, strained, or stopped, try to restore a regular balanced rhythm by inhaling and exhaling through the nose. If the interruption is extreme or you are under a lot of stress, inhale through the nose and exhale out the mouth until balance is restored.

How often are you aware of your breath? What is your average breath like? How deep? How conscious? How relaxed? How regular? What kinds of things cause interruptions to your usual pattern? How often do they occur? How difficult is it to notice when interruptions have occurred? How early do you notice them? How easy is it to recover and restore your breath in various situations?

Over time, just by observing the breath and practicing restoration and recovery, you can learn to calm yourself down, relieve stress, remove pain, and process emotions. Eventually, the process becomes automatic.

BODY SCAN

The physical sense of self is related to identification with patterns of physical and psychological tension. The body has a baseline tension and energy pattern which, when identified with, becomes the feeling of being you. Additional tensions arise through fear, pain, disturbing thoughts and emotions, as well as pleasure, anticipation, desire, and ten-thousand other things. If one becomes attached to these things and identifies with the patterns they create, they become incorporated into the ego. Over time, this pattern of tension and energy can become distorted, out of balance, and unhealthy, affecting breathing, the entire body, and the mind.

Relaxation is the ideal, with any tension needed to maintain form distributed evenly throughout the body, with no blocks in the flow of energy, and no locks in the tissues and joints. Alignment of the spine is such that most of the load can be carried on the body's structure and not through excess muscle tension. When one lies down or is supported, relaxation can be complete.

The body scan exercise is very similar to the breath check, and can be done simultaneously with it. After all, interruptions or restrictions in breathing also reflect increases or imbalances in tension. One will naturally affect the other. This exercise is also a good way to begin a session of meditation.

Practice first by lying down and scanning the body from head to toe, noting any excess tension, pain, or disturbances in the body. Also note any areas where you lack feeling or sensation. If you locate any excess tension or blank spots, on your inhale try to breathe into them, and on the exhale try to release remaining tension. You will probably discover you are not completely relaxed, even though you're lying down and trying to relax. Why is that? What are you holding on to?

Familiarize yourself with any remaining patterns of tension. If you detect lines of tension, breathe into one end of the line and exhale out the other end. If there are just spots or sheets of tension, try breathing in and out of the tension area, or in the tension area and out some other part of the body, or vice versa. In all cases, you are working to increase circulation and free up ingrained patterns of static tension.

Next, try this exercise while lying on each side, on your stomach, and while sitting and standing. Note how alignment and posture affect the patterns of tension in the body. Once you have the basic idea, you can practice this any time throughout the day, noting how movement and stillness, thoughts and emotions, stress and fear, all affect the patterns of tension and energy. Whenever you do this, try to realign your posture by inhaling into any excess tension to correct the alignment, and then releasing the tension on exhale while maintaining form.

For an intensive practice, do a quick body scan every half an hour while you're awake, using breathing and realignment to release all the excess tension you can. Keep it up for a week or two. Eventually, like the breathing, managing and minimizing tension will become automatic. Gradually, the body-mind's tension levels and overall pattern will change.

BODY PERMEATION

These exercises aim at deepening relaxation, removing set tension patterns, and clearing out energy blocks. They also promote blood circulation, regulate blood pressure, develop muscle control, increase body awareness, and lower the overall tone in the nervous system. It is great before or after other exercises, and before or after sleep.

To start, lie down on your back in a comfortable position. On your inhale, gradually tense up all your muscles — try to find every one — so when the inhale is complete, the whole body is tense. On the exhale, gradually relax all your muscles so that when the exhale is complete, the whole body is relaxed. Repeat this a few times.

Next, instead of tensing the whole body all at once on the inhale, tense the muscles starting with the toes, then moving up the legs into the torso and out the arms. Move the line of tension like a wave through the body. When the inhale is complete, the whole body should be tense. On the exhale, the hands relax first and relaxation moves up the arms, down the torso and legs to the feet. After a couple repetitions, reverse the direction, tensing the hands first and relaxing the feet first. Next, try moving the tension through the body in different directions, such as left to right and right to left, front to back and back to front. In each variation, move the line of tension and relaxation like a wave through the body.

These are the basic versions of the exercise, but there are an infinite number of variations. For example, you can focus on tensing just one part of the body with each inhale, such arms, legs, stomach, back, chest — be as specific as you like — and relaxing on the exhale. Or create a spot of tension, and with each inhale and exhale, move the spot of tension to another place on the body.

You can focus on varying the intensity of the tension. Build up to a hundred percent tension, as tense as possible, and then move down ten percent or so with each inhale. At the end, try five percent, then one percent. Finally, just think about tensing on the inhale, and on the exhale release the thought.

You can also speed up the inhale and exhale, or draw it out over longer and longer spans of time. You can try tensing the body into different positions. For example, point the toes and feet, or curl the toes and feet. Make the hands into fists, or spread the fingers. Perform the exercise in different positions, standing, sitting, et cetera.

Start gently in the beginning. You may experience some cramping as muscle imbalances get sorted out and weak muscles attempt to activate. As you progress with the practice, explore as many variations as you can.

Through the exercises, awareness permeates the entire body. Like all the physical exercises, these are not just physical in nature. As ingrained patterns change, look for the process of identification at work. Use the practice as a way to explore the sensations that make up your sense of self, and to stimulate an ongoing inquiry into the nature of the mind, body, and spirit.

MOVEMENT

The possibilities for movement are limitless. I can suggest here only a few basic exercises with rudimentary instructions. However, through your own experimentation, they can form the basis for deep study. Or they can be explored in the context of other movement practices, such as postural yoga, dance, martial arts, or whatever exercise or physical activities you undertake.

I should remind you that while these movement exercises are great for general health and well-being, as a spiritual practice, careful observation and inquiry is important. During practice we may gain insight into our fear, impatience, selfishness, desires, anger, arrogance, ambitions, and pain. Open yourself to acknowledging whatever arises and using it as a starting point for inquiry. With that in mind, here is a general practice.

Beginning from a standing position, lay down on the ground and get back up again. Do this as many different ways as you can manage. Don't rush. Take as much time as you need. Try to move smoothly and at a consistent speed. Avoid excessive tension, beyond what is required for the movement. The point is to observe what happens when you move, where tension arises, if there is any difficulty, where you hold your breath, and any other sensations, thoughts, or emotions that arise.

Next, add specific breathing patterns. From standing, begin to inhale and start moving downward. Halfway down, begin to exhale. Finish exhaling as your movement finishes and you're lying down. Then, begin another inhale and start moving upward. Halfway up begin to exhale and complete exhaling as you finish standing up. If this is too difficult, try two full breaths down and two full breaths up. Continue lying down and getting up with continuous movement and breathing. Practice every day until you feel that you could sustain it indefinitely without having to catch your breath or recover at the end.

Next, push the breathing further. From a standing position, exhale and go down, completing the exhale in a lying-down position. Inhale and stand up, completing the inhale in a standing position. The breath rate should be smooth and steady throughout the movement. Practice this for a while, catching your breath as needed, and then push further. On the inhale go down and stand up, and on the exhale go down and stand up. Then, go down and up twice on the inhale and down and up twice on the exhale. If you can, do three or more! No matter how much breath and movement control you have, eventually your breathing will become unbalanced and feel inadequate. Struggle with this for a while, then catch your breath and go back to an easier version, like exhale down and inhale up. Keep practicing at various levels, and pushing at higher levels, until you feel comfortable automatically balancing breathing and movement to sustain the activity.

Always observe what's happening in your body and what difficulties you have. One key to this exercise is focusing on the timing and balance of the breath rather than the movement. Try to lead with the breath by starting the inhale or exhale just before the movement. Visualize the breath going ahead of you, down or up, and simply follow it with your movement. Remember, don't rush. There's no hurry. You're not going to get anywhere, just down and up again.

One variation is to add crawling on the ground while you are down and walking while you are up. For example, you might try exhale down, inhale crawl, exhale stand up, inhale walk. Or you may simply want to walk, inhale one step, exhale one step, inhale two steps, exhale two steps, then three steps, four steps, and so on. Do as many as you can do and then go back down again.

Another variation is to do any of the exercises with your eyes closed. Yet another is to base your movement solely on an unpremeditated, involuntary breath cycle. In this variation, simply breathe as needed and watch the breath. When you're exhaling, move as if you're on your way to lying down. When you are inhaling, move as if you're on your way to standing up. Don't worry if you get all the way down or all the way up. Just follow the breath.

From here you can create as many variations you want, practice linking breath to any other kind of movement, or just go down and up. It's a wonderful practice that will keep you mobile into old age, while providing the potential for deep insight.

STILLNESS

If you're practicing sitting meditation, you're probably already working on stillness to some extent, but let's make physical stillness the real focus here. Lie down, get comfortable, and then don't move at all for five or ten minutes. You can breathe of course, and you will blink if your eyes are open, but that's it. Don't move anything else, no matter how tempting it is. Observe all the mental activity that takes place in this stillness, be it thoughts or desires, pain or pleasure, fear or anxiety … whatever it is. Pay particular attention to the sensation you have of being in your body. Notice your awareness of various body parts and the feeling of occupying them. Note any changes to your sensations and awareness during the exercise.

That's the basic practice. Now let's add a few variations. In the first variation, listen to and feel the activity inside your body. There's a lot going on despite the external stillness. Listen to each breath go into and out of the lungs. Listen for any movement in the digestive system. Then listen for your heart beat. See if you can feel your pulse internally in different parts of your body — in the chest, stomach, legs, feet, hands, head, back, and so on. If you're able to do this, then try to feel the pulse everywhere all at once. See if you can feel the heart beat and a full-body pulse. Feel the blood flow out and back with each heartbeat. Then try to synchronize heartbeat with breathing, at first by counting — three beats inhale, three beats exhale. Finally, see if you can allow synchronization to find its own pace and just watch it all happen.

In the next variation, close your eyes and pay attention to the sensation you have of occupying your whole body. Then practice moving your awareness, focusing it into different parts of the body — chest, stomach, legs, feet, hands, back, front of the head, back of the head, and so on. When you feel you have some control over this, fill the whole body with your awareness again. Then, on the exhale, expand your awareness a little beyond the limits of the body. On the inhale, contract your awareness inward until it is a little smaller than the limits of the body. Continue like this, expanding and contracting the awareness, occasionally reversing which you are doing on inhale and exhale.

Next, regardless of the breath, expand your awareness more and more until it feels as big as it can get. Then do the opposite, contracting the awareness so it collapses within the body, smaller and smaller, abandoning the limbs and extremities, and more and more of the body, until it is just a tiny point deep inside. Experiment with where to place this point — in the abdomen, the chest, the front of the head, the back of the head, and so on. When it has settled somewhere, let go of all control over your awareness and just observe whatever happens. Let go and enter a state of open awareness.

For further variations, you can do these exercises in different positions and for varying lengths of time. You can experiment with doing them before or after physical exercise and at different times throughout the day. Feeling the internal heartbeat, for example, can be significantly easier just after exercise when the heart is pumping more vigorously. There are many things to discover within this relative stillness.

PROCESSING PAIN

Of all the negative experiences one can have, including the entire spectrum of negative thoughts, emotions, and sensations, pain is perhaps the most immediate and visceral. For this reason it can be quite instructive and will serve as a model for processing and transforming any negative experience. Once you understand the basics of breathing, acceptance, and direct gazing, you can apply this practice of processing pain to negative thoughts, emotions, or sensations as needed.

Breathing is the first principle. When pain arises, especially if it does so suddenly, it usually disrupts breathing. A person may hold their breath, cry, or even scream. To begin processing the pain it is important to restore balanced breathing. As soon as pain arises, begin focused breathing by inhaling through the nose and exhaling out the mouth. If the pain is extreme, rapid shallow breathing may continue to make this possible. If the body doubles over or muscles spasm and clench up, breathing is further inhibited. If possible, open yourself up, and try to relax your muscles. As you inhale, visualize breathing into the pain, wherever it is. As you exhale, visualize exhaling the pain from your body.

Acceptance is the second principle. Once pain is present, it cannot be avoided. This seems to go without saying, but people will seek any chance to escape, ignore, repress, or otherwise avoid processing pain directly. Acceptance does not mean you should not take any action, for example, to remove your hand from a hot stove. But any pain that is present is already happening, and anything other than complete acceptance is at odds with the actuality of what is. Any attempt to escape or wish it weren't so will create a separation and an imaginary conflict which only causes further suffering. Work toward accepting present pain. The pain may be guiding you to move or lay down or rest in order to heal yourself. Without acceptance you will not hear or heed this guidance toward healing.

Direct gazing is the third principle. Instead of trying to distract yourself by looking away from the pain or thinking about something else, turn the gaze of your awareness directly on the pain itself. Do not be afraid of it. Look right at it, and see it for what it is. Pure sensation! Everything else is just a cascade of thoughts and emotions, hopes and fears, drawing you into an imaginary past or future, which is the actual cause of any suffering. By your direct gaze, pain is transformed into presence, the unadorned awareness of what is.

One difficulty with this exercise is that pain must be present. Therefore, seize any opportunity for practice. For the sake of our practice, fortunately opportunities are not usually in short supply. You may have an injury, a headache, a stomach ache, or a nagging pain. You might accidentally stub a toe or cut a finger. All are opportunities for practice.

Beyond opportunistic practice, deep-tissue massage is another way to practice processing pain. Not only will you get to practice, but the practice will increase the depth and effect of the massage. Instruction for massage is beyond our scope here, but one technique that's easy to use is to lie face down and have someone step on your calves. They should start gently, slowly applying pressure, and gradually go deeper and deeper as you practice processing any pain that arises.

You can also apply the practice to whatever negative experience arises in the context of your life. I have chosen to discuss pain here because of its acute, visceral, and immediate nature. But there's no reason you couldn't begin practice with negative thoughts, emotions, memories, self-chatter, fear, anxiety, or any stress response or negative sensation. The basic principles are exactly the same: breathing, acceptance, and direct gazing.

If the pain you're working with is intense or overwhelming, you don't have to take it on all at once. Work on processing the outer edges first and deal with it in layers. Physical sensations may be tied into emotions, thoughts, and other deeper sensations. It may take time, but gradually move toward a gaze that can see everything, all the layers and forms of pain all at once. Ultimately, the very suffering and confusion of the deluded mind can be transformed into enlightenment.

DEVOTION & PRAYER

If you follow a traditional path or are drawn to one, some kind of devotion or prayer may already be part of your spiritual practice. If so, you can go deeper into it. If not, and you wish to explore this type of practice, it isn't difficult to get started. Don't be intimidated by the ornamental complexities of religions and their formal practices. Devotion and prayer may not always be easy, but their essence is natural and intuitive.

There's no point worrying about which religion is right. For people of every faith and of no faith at all, from beginning to end, there is only what is, and it is all encompassing. Not only do all religions and all the names of God point toward that, but every leaf, every star, every person, every mote of dust, every atom, every thought, every action, absolutely everything points toward that. Because God so exceeds our every conception is precisely why we must strive to make contact. If it was as easy as giving a name to the nameless, we would all be saints already.

So now that we've cleared that up, let's get on with it.

The general practice here is to quiet the mind and let go of the self by focusing on a love and longing for God alone. Your concept of God may be very personal and specific or mind-bogglingly abstract. Either way, it is still a form or image. And the basic idea is that you accept this image of the divine as the object of your devotion and prayer.

Of course, God is beyond any concept, form, or image, but God is also present in all forms. So an image of God can help focus one's efforts toward the divine. The essence of devotion is simply falling in love with this image, and I can offer you no advice on that, other than if it happens, to sacrifice more and more of yourself for the sake of this love, and to allow your conception of God to grow until it encompasses everything. Before this love blooms, however, devotion consists in remembering God, and the struggle to understand God's image and one's relation to it.

Some devotional practices, such as adoration, praise, gratitude, and supplication, are open to all and require little by way of explanation. Others, such as rituals and worship, are perhaps best explored through existing religious traditions. A few practices may occupy a middle-ground, open to all, and yet requiring some direction.

One devotional practice is the surrender of personal will. Whatever wishes, hopes, and desire you may have, whatever predictions for the future you entertain, give up your desire to control all these things. In your mind, turn your life over to God. Take action as needed, but practice really accepting whatever happens as God's will, the divine unfolding, or whatever you want to call it. Even when something is beyond your understanding, that too give up to God.

One prayer practice is the repetition of sacred words. Choose a short prayer or mantra that focuses your intention on reaching the divine and surrendering the self. Repeat the words as a way of quieting your thoughts, reinforcing your intention, and sustaining your attention, as in meditation. Continue to repeat these words in quiet moments and whenever troubling thoughts or situations assail you. Synchronize the words with your breath, and even your heartbeat, repeating them until they seem to come effortlessly and continue endlessly in the background of your awareness.

The mystical and contemplative traditions of various religions are rich resources for deepening one's understanding of these practices. However, it's important to note that devotional and prayer practices are ultimately no different than other practices. In the end, our hearts must break, for we must still give everything up, including our image of God. Ultimately, we will still have to cut through all the delusions of a separate ego-self and see through all distinctions between self, other, God, and world.

CONTEMPLATION

Doubt is the engine of spiritual contemplation. To really look thoughtfully at anything, first discard all preconceptions and beliefs. Take nothing for granted. As a spiritual practice, look upon the object of any contemplation with open, clear eyes, unattached to any predetermined conclusion. Sit comfortably in unknowing and ever-deeper wonder. True insight cannot be forced, rushed, or grabbed at.

Spiritual contemplation is more than just thinking about something. Although you may engage in thought, remain distrustful of it. Thoughts are only things, and could themselves be the objects of contemplation. From where do they arise? How are you aware of them? And so on. Whatever the object of your contemplation, you are seeking insight into what lies beyond thought. Stay committed to nothing less than what is real and true.

What is really going on? What is it that you are actually experiencing?

Anything could be the object of contemplation if approached in this spirit of truth seeking. But as a spiritual practice, certain things tend to be particularly well suited for contemplation. A short list might include the nature of objects themselves, the nature of time, birth and death, perception, impermanence, and the self.

If you've been following a traditional path in your spiritual life, the depths of contemplation is no place to rely on doctrine. Buddhists should forget about the Buddha. Christians should stop just believing in Christ. And so on. How else are you going to *be* the Buddha that you have been from the beginning? How else are you going to recognize the Christ who has always been with you? How else will you realize God if you continue to believe that God is elsewhere? How else will you know what you really are unless you stop believing that you are anything at all? Risk everything! How else are you going to discover for yourself what's true?

If you have a philosophical or scientific outlook, try to expose the core fundamental assumptions upon which you base all your thinking. Face the fact that without certainty there, while your endeavors may be incredibly useful, they are essentially worthless with regard to finding the absolute truth. Try to unmask the illusions inherent in your conceptual understanding. If you're working on difficult, complex, or new ideas, try writing them down to help clarify your thinking.

Contemplation is the sometimes painful task of trying, with complete honesty, to separate delusion from truth, to separate what you think you know from direct contact with the unknown. It is in the end, a process of completely emptying the self.

When the object of contemplation is phrased as a question, the practice takes the form of an inquiry. Still, the point is not to figure it out and answer the question. Look beyond any concept-based answers that come to mind. Sit quietly with the question, and wait for insight to arise.

For example, contemplating the nature of the self, you might ask: Who or what is contemplating? Who is it who desires? Who is afraid? Who is asking these questions? Who or what are you, really? This question goes right to the heart of it all. Seek the truth unrelentingly, with complete honesty, and without ever settling for anything less than what is absolutely real. Because no matter what you think or believe or say now, when you go beyond thought, beyond belief, beyond all words, to realize the truth, you're in for a big surprise.

EMULATING SELFLESSNESS

This kind of practice focuses on emulating the attitudes and states that arise from enlightenment. Doing this creates opportunities to realize innate selflessness. Mystics throughout the ages have shown clearly where to put your attention in such a practice. You might start by cultivating these four attitudes: loving kindness, compassion, empathetic joy, and equanimity. I'll discuss each one briefly and how you might endeavor to practice.

Loving kindness is active love and good will toward others. Imagine the most benevolent, unconditional, selfless love you can — like that of a devoted parent toward a child perhaps, only more selfless. Now extend this love to everyone and all beings. Call to mind specific people, including those you don't like, those who repulse you, who you don't agree with, who have injured you, or who are your enemies, and extend this loving kindness toward them. As you go about your day, be attentive to this feeling. There are many opportunities to let this good will guide your everyday actions.

Compassion is feeling the suffering of others as your own. To practice compassion, you need only look around and really recognize the suffering of others, big and small. Look at other people, and see that their hopes and fears, their pains and longings, their frustration, anger, and confusion are no different than yours. Feel the longing to ease all suffering as you would ease your own. Again, call to mind specific people. It's important to practice compassion for those you don't like, those who repulse you, who you don't agree with, who have injured you, or who are your enemies. In the light of compassion there is no room for discrimination. We all share the same suffering.

Empathetic joy is feeling the joy of others as your own. To practice, first be attentive to joy itself. Try to recognize and cultivate joy in yourself. Imagine a time when you were filled with joy. Remember what it felt like, and try to evoke that feeling in yourself. Can you find joy in this present moment? Now, when you imagine the happiness of another, or recognize joy in others you encounter, find this joy within yourself and realize its sameness. When you really see that there is no separation between self and other, the joy of others is truly your joy.

Equanimity can be thought of as even-mindedness, composure, tolerance, serenity, and peace. To practice equanimity, first observe your mind to see what disturbs it. You may think you already know, but it's quite a different thing when you observe your thoughts and emotions in the process of being disturbed. Get in the habit of noticing when this happens early in the process, so you have an opportunity to intervene. When you make inner peace a priority, however, you can't force the matter by repressing disturbing thoughts or emotions, nor can you give them free reign. Everything must be clear to you.

Many of the practices discussed already will help. Meditation will teach you to be an observer of your thoughts and emotions without getting caught up in them. Processing pain and transforming negative thoughts and emotions will teach you how to intervene. Contemplating the impermanence of all mental states will teach you perspective. And in the immediate presence of a real threat to your composure, practice focused breathing. Of course, take action as necessary, but do so with a calm mind.

These attitudes complement each other. Practicing one will help cultivate all four. They are intimately interconnected, with each one leading to the others. That is because ultimately, they are all the same. They are all manifestations of selfless being. Ultimately, you cannot make yourself more loving or compassionate or composed. It is only by surrendering the self that such natural aspects of consciousness are revealed.

A variation on this type of practice, common among many spiritual traditions, is to follow some kind of moral code or set of precepts. In this case, the code is a guide to emulating selflessness. The ongoing conflict with the code, from within and without, and the struggle to understand and maintain it, serves to disrupt and challenge the boundaries of the ego-self.

SOLITUDE

It is no coincidence that many of the ancient masters wandered alone in the mountains, or ventured into the desert, or lived in caves for years on end. Solitude can help bring one face to face with one's true nature. As a spiritual practice solitude can reveal unexamined attachments, the limits of the ego, and oneness with the total environment.

It is not necessary to live the life of a recluse, or to dwell alone in a cave for half your life. But to really know solitude is to know oneself, and that is truly invaluable.

Practicing solitude is really the simplest thing, but many people in modern society find it difficult. So find time to go off by yourself, as far from other people as you can. Leave behind your laptop and your phone, and any other gadgets that will distract you from experiencing solitude. If you want a phone for emergencies, at least turn it off and pack it away where you won't be tempted to use it.

Although one can practice solitude anywhere, there is something about a quiet place away from town that is ideal. There is nothing like encountering the wilderness to make clear how connected we are to nature, and to put you in contact with your own suffering. And there is nothing like the natural world to reveal instantly the beauty and the bliss of being.

Just get away. Lose yourself. Go for a day, a weekend, or longer if you can manage. Plan to devote yourself to spiritual seeking, or plan nothing at all. Just finding some solitude can be enough. Listen to the sound of the wind in the trees. Watch the ever-changing clouds as they move across the sky. Contemplate the endless waves as they crash upon the shore. Therein, perhaps you will find peace.

Silence

Finally, with regard to practice, I would like to say something about silence. For perhaps nothing comes so close to the truth as this. And nothing comes so close to the nature of delusion as the constant chatter of people, within and without. The mind is a tangle of repetitious, clamoring, obsessive thoughts, and in the world these thoughts find voice in the endless conversations and activities of everyday life.

To practice silence, for a day or a week, even in the context of one interaction or a single instant, creates space for the recognition of consciousness at work. In silence, one can bring some of the peace of solitude into everyday life.

You can begin your practice by taking a day off from speaking. Let any people you live with know what you're up to, and give your mouth and your mind a rest. This will give you a taste of silence. Observe its effects on you, your thoughts, and your interactions with others. If you have the time and can manage it, try a few days or a week. It's not as difficult as you might imagine, and the benefits can be profound.

In your everyday life, while at work, at home, and while out and about, you can continue to practice silence by refraining from unnecessary, frivolous, and especially negative or harmful speech. When you're in a conversation, whether at a meeting or with friends, all kinds of thoughts and speech impulses may arise. What is your motivation for speaking? What will be the effects of your words? Do you really need to speak? Or is this an opportunity to practice silence?

Silence itself is an opportunity to practice meditation in everyday moments. Instead of speaking, observe what's really happening in the mind as it formulates thoughts to voice. Observe the people you are with, and try to see the origins of their words and the true nature of the conversation.

For a deeper practice, do not stop at a silent voice. Cultivate silent eyes, silent ears, a silent mind, a silent body, and a silent heart. This holy silence is the opening through which realization can enter.

Additional Practices

Thousands of years of traditions have given us many worthwhile practices, and there are many resources available today. I encourage you to seek these out if interested. But beware of being a mere collector of experiences, or of clinging to the technical or conceptual aspects of a tradition or practice. Seek depth in practice, even more than breadth. Ultimately, the practices and traditions will themselves have to be transcended.

Many teachings offer detailed instruction on meditation and contemplation that go far beyond the scope of this book. It can be helpful to experience guided meditations, learn of the difficulties other practitioners have faced, and get answers to questions that arise. There are numerous teachers, books, workshops, retreats, and even apps devoted solely to meditation practice.

Postural yoga is very popular and can be readily explored through books, classes, apps, and videos. These physical practices are incredibly beneficial to health and well-being, and were originally developed as an integral component of meditation, devotion, and inquiry. Yoga can be an effective method of creating space in the body and mind, and a great way to deepen your breathing, movement, and meditation practices.

My own most consistent practice through many years has been martial arts. And although this won't appeal to everyone, I will say the following. Many people get into martial arts with a variety of delusions about what they're doing and why. Even after years of training, many martial artists look at the practice as a way for peaceful people to learn how to cope with violence. But as a spiritual practice, it is exactly the opposite. Ultimately, it is a way for violent people to learn how to cope with peace. It is a way for those already in conflict with themselves to find a way to let go of fighting, and to embrace the love and compassion that is ever present.

Finally I would like to say that whatever you take up in life could be a spiritual practice. Whether you are doing the dishes, gardening, walking the dog, cleaning the house, working at your job, or engaging in a hobby, give your full attention to the present moment. Observe what is before you. Be aware of your sensations, thoughts, and emotions. If you notice you are distracted, gently bring your attention back to the present moment and whatever it is you are doing. In truth, there is not a single moment that is not a part of this spiritual journey.

Teachers and Gurus

Many people seek out a teacher for direct spiritual advice and guidance with practices, or for instruction on practices such as meditation, yoga, massage and healing, or even martial arts. There is no doubt that a good teacher, even one who is not enlightened, can be a great blessing in one's life, and help prepare one for awakening.

If you are searching for a teacher, do some homework and be open to the possibilities. There is no need to commit to any teacher unless you feel you can benefit from their teachings. And there is no real reason why you can't explore different teachings or have several teachers simultaneously or over time.

I would feel remiss if I didn't give some word of caution here to those seeking spiritual instruction. All one has to do is survey the history of various cults, spiritual movements, and self-help fads to see that from a desire for spiritual experience or understanding, people can be led deeper into delusion.

An unskeptical person, a desperate person, or a person whose psychological makeup craves authoritarian control, belief, or a subservient role can easily fall prey to manipulation. Unscrupulous people, and even well-meaning people in the depths of their own delusions, can and do use spiritual trappings, ideas, and concepts for their own ego-driven desires.

You need not give up your faculty for critical thinking or good judgment to proceed on a spiritual path. In fact, to seek the truth it is vital that you exercise them. If you are searching for a teacher or engaged with any teaching, you are the final authority for yourself and your spiritual practice. There is no other way.

Of course, in the midst of our delusion, clarity is not always forthcoming. Even a fully-enlightened person may not appear to you to be anything special. And if you don't know anything about a particular practice, how would you know a good teacher if you saw one?

As in all things, you just do the best you can. What else can you do? Overall, a good teacher will be a good person, in addition to having some skill or knowledge. An awakened teacher will consistently embody the selfless truth. Although some may employ strange methods, or even appear to have some vices or faults, the fruits of their awakening will be evident over time. The continual presence of deep peace, compassion, joy, and honesty are perhaps the best guidelines you have to go by.

THE END OF ALL THINGS

There is an end to all things. When you reach it, you'll be ready to wake up. It's as simple as that. At that time, let go of all your treasured beliefs, every shred of meaning or desire that you cling to, and any idea or concept that seems to hold your life and world together. The ego-self and all external objects will pass away into nothing. It all comes to an end.

For all such structures are inherently unstable. At best, they are like fortresses built on shifting sands. They are like castles in the sky, and no amount of propping them up will endure. Seen more clearly, they are like wisps of smoke in the air, like drops of rain in a vast ocean. All conditioned phenomena are thus, like the most fleeting images imaginable.

And so all your practices, whatever they may be, must too be seen in this light. They all come to an end. Although they may go on for other reasons, all fail to bring about enlightenment. They are only to help you along the way. Eventually, they too will be transcended. And it is their very failures that may bring you to the doorstep of awakening.

Ultimately, there is no distinction between meditation and everyday life. There is no distinction between contemplation and silence, or between processing pain and movement, or even between movement and stillness. There is no distinction between mind and body, body and spirit. There are no distinctions whatsoever!

So free yourself of everything, and awaken to the boundless blissful beautiful truth that is before you now.

APPENDIX A

PRACTICES OUTLINE

The following outline summarizes the practices discussed in this book. Use it as a reminder and quick reference. Pick a practice and focus on it for a while with consistency. Establish your intention, take note of contrast, conduct ongoing inquiry, and remember that you are responsible for your own practice and where it takes you.

Beginning Meditation

1. Sit with good posture.
2. Breathe and relax.
3. Be aware of what is.

Logistics: Take a few deep breaths at the beginning, releasing excess tension, and allow some time at the end to let the mind go.

Sustaining Attention

1. Begin meditation.
2. Focus your attention on the breath.
3. If you notice the attention has strayed, gently return your attention to the breath.

Variation: Focus your attention on some other object of meditation, such as a candle, a rock, a mantra, or a sacred image.

Variation: When the attention strays, note the distraction as a thought, an emotion, or a sensation, before gently returning your attention to the breath.

Observing Thoughts

1. Begin meditation.
2. Observe your thoughts as they come and go.
3. If you become caught up in thoughts, see what happened and gently return your attention to observing the thoughts as they come and go.

Variation: Observe your emotions or sensations.

Open Awareness

1. Begin meditation.
2. Practice selective awareness of sounds, sights, tastes, smells, bodily sensations, thoughts, and emotions, without labeling or analyzing.
3. Without directing your attention in any way, open your awareness to the entire field of perception in which various phenomena arise and fall away, without resistance or grasping.

Note: This can form the backbone of ongoing meditation practice.

Seeing Nothing

1. Begin meditation.
2. Stop all thoughts, and do not allow the attention to focus on anything whatsoever.
3. If anything arises in awareness, gently abandon it and return the attention to nothing.

Note: Use as an occasional practice to return to periodically.

Breath Exploration

1. Observe your breathing.
2. Consciously control several breath cycles through voluntary action.
3. Let go of conscious breath control and observe involuntary breathing in action.

Continuation: Switch between voluntary and involuntary breathing. Make voluntary breathing more subtle until you can identify the dividing line between voluntary and involuntary.

Variation: With voluntary breathing, breathe into various parts of the body. With involuntary breathing, observe where the breath goes.

Breath Suspension

1. Lie down, inhale, exhale, and hold the breath with neutral air pressure.
2. Observe all reactions and thoughts as the breath hold continues.
3. Breathe in through the nose and out the mouth and continue your observations as the body completely recovers.

Variation: Try lying on each side and on the stomach.

Breath Check

1. Periodically check in with your breathing throughout the day.
2. Pay attention to anything that may disrupt or stop the pattern of regular breathing.
3. Whenever you notice an interruption, try to restore a balanced rhythm by inhaling and exhaling through the nose. In more extreme cases, inhale through the nose and exhale out the mouth.

Variation: Combine with a body scan.

Body Scan

1. Scan the body from head to toe.
2. Note any areas of excess tension or pain, as well as blank spots or dead zones.
3. Inhale into trouble spots and try to release any excess tension on the exhale.

Variation: Combine with a periodic breath check.

Body Permeation

1. Lie down and get in a comfortable position.
2. On the inhale, gradually tense up all your muscles so that you are completely tense, head to toe, as you finish your inhale.
3. On the exhale, gradually relax all your muscles so that you are completely relaxed, head to toe, as you finish your exhale.

Variation: With the breath, tense and relax the body in a variety of wavelike patterns.

Movement

1. Starting from a standing position, lay down on the ground and stand back up again.
2. Do this in as many different ways as you can manage.
3. Add specific breathing, such as inhale-exhale down and inhale-exhale up, or exhale down and inhale up, or inhale down and up and exhale down and up.

Variation: Add crawling while on the ground and walking while standing.

Variation: Practice with eyes closed.

Variation: Follow involuntary breath cycle down on exhale, up on inhale.

STILLNESS

1. Lie down, get comfortable, and don't move for five or ten minutes.
2. Note the feeling of being inside your body.
3. Note any changes to that feeling during practice.

Variation: Feel the pulse inside the body and recognize full-body pulse. Allow pulse and breathing to synchronize.

Variation: Move the awareness to different areas of the body, then expand and contract awareness outward and inward from the limits of the body.

PROCESSING PAIN

1. Use proportionate focused breathing to relax yourself and restore balanced breathing.
2. Accept present pain. Don't feel sorry for yourself. Don't engage in psychological avoidance.
3. Turn the gaze of awareness directly on the pain itself. Look right at it, and see it as pure sensation.

Variation: Process extensive or overwhelming pain in layers. Start with the outer edges and work inward to its root.

Note: This practice can be used to process any negative thoughts, emotions, or sensations.

Devotion & Prayer

1. Choose an image of God and struggle to understand and expand your conception of it.
2. Surrender your will and self to God
3. Repeat a prayer or mantra.

Continuation: Focus on a love and longing for God alone. Synchronize prayer repetition with breath and heartbeat.

Contemplation

1. Doubt everything and ask questions in a relentless search for the truth.
2. When engaging in thought, maintain robust skepticism in the face of any idea, concept, or story.
3. Sit with a sense of unknowing and the unknown, while you wait for insight to arise.

Variation: Write down your thoughts. Try to determine what assumptions they are based on and if they are true.

Emulating Selflessness

1. Approach loving kindness, compassion, empathetic joy, and equanimity with a spirit of inquiry. What are they and can you recognize them in yourself?
2. Try to recognize these attitudes in your interactions and observations.
3. Try to allow these attitudes to guide your actions in everyday life.

Variation: Commit yourself to following a set of spiritual precepts.

Solitude

1. Go off by yourself.
2. Turn off your gadgets.
3. Enjoy your being.

Variation: Dedicate yourself to a disciplined set of practices.

Silence

1. Take some time off from speaking.
2. Observe the effects of silence on you and your interactions with others.
3. Look for opportunities to practice silence in everyday moments.

Variation: Study the speech and silence of others to understand what is really going on.

APPENDIX B

BIBLIOGRAPHY

I have alluded to a few well-known poems and passages within the text, but have otherwise endeavored to root everything in my direct and immediate insight. Nevertheless, I've read a number of books related to spirituality, practices, and enlightenment — before and after awakening — and they have certainly influenced my choice of topics and use of words. Influence is wonderfully unavoidable, and as it may be helpful for you to know what some of these influences have been, I am including a bibliography, which could also serve as a recommended reading list. As such, I will include a few books I read after writing this one, but which I found particularly worthwhile. If you take up any of these texts, I trust you will enjoy them as much as I did.

Adyashanti, *The End of Your World,* Sounds True, 2010.

Adyashanti, *The Way of Liberation,* Open Gate Sangha, 2012.

Alexandra David-Neel and Lama Yongden, *The Secret Oral Teachings in Tibetan Buddhist Sects,* Important Books, 2013.

Anandamayi Ma, *The Essential Sri Anandamayi Ma: Life and Teachings of a 20th Century Indian Saint,* Edited by Joseph A. Fitzgerald, Biography by Alexander Lipski & Words of Anandamayi Ma, World Wisdom, 2007.

The Dhammapada, Lost Edition.

Peter Haskel, *Bankei Zen: Translations from The Record of Bankei,* Edited by Yoshito Hakeda, Grove Weidenfeld, 1984.

Richard Hittleman, *Guide to Yoga Meditation,* Bantam Books, 1969.

Alejandro Jodorowsky, *Psychomagic: The Transformative Power of Shamanic Psychotherapy,* Translated by Rachael LeValley, Inner Traditions, 2010.

Konstantin Komarov, *Systema Manual: Practical and Fundamental Training Guide,* Translated by Dimitri Trufanov, Systema Headquarters, 2014.

Wolfgang Kopp, *Free Yourself of Everything: Radical Guidance in the Spirit of Zen and Christian Mysticism,* Translated by Barbara Wittenberg-Hasenauer, Tuttle Library of Enlightenment, 1994.

Wolfgang Kopp, *Zen: Beyond all Words,* Translated by Barbara Wittenberg-Hasenauer, Tuttle Library of Enlightenment, 1996.

Thomas Keating, *Open Mind Open Heart: The Contemplative Dimension of the Gospel*, Continuum, 2004.

J. Krishnamurti, *Freedom from the Known*, Edited by Mary Lutyens, Harper & Row, 1969.

Sri Nisargadatta Maharaj, *I Am That: Talks with Nisargadatta Maharaj*, Translated by Maurice Frydman, Edited by Sudhakar S. Dikshit, The Acorn Press, 2012.

Sri Ramana Maharshi, *Be As You Are: The Teachings of Sri Ramana Maharshi*, Edited by David Godman, Penguin Arkana, 1985.

Sri Ramana Maharshi, *Talks with Sri Ramana Maharshi*, transcribed by Munagala Venkataramiah, Sri Ramanasramam, 2016.

Sri Ramana Maharshi, *The Collected Works of Ramana Maharshi*, Edited by Arthur Osborne, Weiser Books, 1997.

Joel Morwood, *Naked Through the Gate: A Spiritual Autobiography*, Center for Sacred Sciences, 1985.

Joel Morwood, *The Way of Selflessness: A Practical Guide to Enlightenment Based on the Teachings of the World's Great Mystics*, Center for Sacred Sciences, 2009.

Mumon's Gateless Gate, Lost Edition.

Miyamoto Musashi, *The Book of Five Rings*, Translated by Thomas Cleary, Shambhala Dragon Editions, 1993.

Takuan Soho, *The Unfettered Mind: Writings from a Zen Master to a Master Swordsman*, Translated by William Scott Wilson, Shambhala, 2012.

Eckhart Tolle, *The Power of Now: A Guide to Spiritual Enlightenment*, Namaste Publishing, 2004.

Chogyam Trungpa, *Cutting Through Spiritual Materialism*, Shambhala Classics, 2002.

Chogyam Trungpa, *Training the Mind and Cultivating Loving-Kindness*, Shambhala Classics, 1993.

Chuang Tsu, *Inner Chapters*, Translated by Gia-Fu Feng and Jane English, Vintage Books, 1974.

Lao Tsu, *Tao Te Ching*, Translated by Gia-Fu Feng and Jane English, Vintage Books, 1972/2011.

Morihei Ueshiba, *The Art of Peace*, Translated and Edited by John Stevens, Shambhala Classics, 2002.

The Holy Bible: Containing the Old and New Testaments, Revised Standard Version, Ignatius Press, 1966.

The Upanishads, Translated by Vernon Katz and Thomas Egenes, Jeremy P. Tarcher/Penguin, 2015.

Vladimir Vasiliev with Scott Meredith, *Let Every Breath: Secrets of the Russian Breath Masters*, Systema Headquarters, 2006.

Alan Watts, *The Wisdom of Insecurity*, Vintage Books, 2011.

Alan Watts, *The Way of Zen*, Vintage Books, 1999.

Alan Watts, *Out of Your Mind: Essential Listening from the Alan Watts Audio Archives*, Sounds True, 2004.

Franklin Merrell-Wolff, *Experience and Philosophy: A Personal Record of Transformation and a Discussion of Transcendental Consciousness*, SUNY press, 1994.

ABOUT THE AUTHOR

On April 11th, 2016 Matthew Lowes had an unexpected and profound spiritual awakening, just as the great mystics have described. Since this enlightenment dawned, he has endeavored to communicate the insights intrinsic to realization and to help others on their spiritual journey. In addition to this work, he continues to be a writer of fiction and games, as well as a student and teacher of martial arts, fitness, and health practices.

matthewlowes.com

The spiritual journey is your life exactly as it is.

WHEN YOU ARE SILENT IT SPEAKS

MATTHEW LOWES

CHARTING THE SPIRITUAL PATH

An exploration of the spiritual journey: from the suffering of our
existential hopes and fears, through a search for the truth,
to the unimaginable awakening that awaits us all.

— Coming in 2021

Thank you for reading!

Please post a review online. :)

The next book in this series,
When You are Silent It Speaks,
is coming in 2021.

Made in the USA
Columbia, SC
11 May 2020

96202434R00138